UNDER THE SOCIALIST BANNER

Cover photo and frontispiece: Opening session at 1904 congress of Second International in Amsterdam. Banner in Dutch reads: "Proletarians of all lands, unite!" Among those at speakers' table: Clara Zetkin (second from left, standing and translating), Rosa Luxemburg (fifth from left), Sen Katayama (sixth from left), Hendrick Van Kol (seventh from left), and Georgy Plekhanov (ninth from left). Photographer: Corn. Leenheer. From International Institute of Social History (Amsterdam), call number BG D1/389.

UNDER THE SOCIALIST BANNER

RESOLUTIONS OF THE SECOND INTERNATIONAL, 1889–1912

Edited by Mike Taber

Haymarket Books
Chicago, IL

Published in 2021 by
Haymarket Books
P.O. Box 180165
Chicago, IL 60618
773-583-7884
www.haymarketbooks.org
info@haymarketbooks.org

ISBN: 978-1-64259-467-6

Distributed to the trade in the US through Consortium Book Sales and
Distribution (www.cbsd.com) and internationally through Ingram Publisher
Services International (www.ingramcontent.com).

This book was published with the generous support of Lannan Foundation and
Wallace Action Fund.

Special discounts are available for bulk purchases by organizations and institutions. Please email orders@haymarketbooks.org for more information.

Cover design by Eric Kerl.

Printed in Canada.

Library of Congress Cataloging-in-Publication data is available.

10 9 8 7 6 5 4 3 2 1

CONTENTS

APPROVED RESOLUTIONS BY THEME

Jewish question

Labor legislation and workers' conditions

Trade unions

Trusts

Women's emancipation

Introduction

Socialism.

That word—considered by some to have been relegated to dusty historical archives—has once again become a major point of contention in contemporary politics. So much so that US president Donald Trump regularly conjured up the socialist bogeyman as he sought to justify some of the more reactionary policies of his administration. By doing this, however, Trump inadvertently testified to the massive growth of interest in socialism today, especially among young people.

An Axios poll in early 2019 found that 61 percent of US citizens age eighteen to twenty-four viewed socialism in a favorable light. Such sentiment is remarkable given the decades of Cold War antisocialist rhetoric that has inundated US political culture. Another indication of the deepening interest in socialism is the explosive growth of the Democratic Socialists of America, whose membership jumped from six thousand in 2016 to well over ten times that number by early 2020.

Behind this phenomenon of socialism's growing appeal is the dawning recognition by millions of young people and others that capitalism offers them no future. Millions are saddled with student debt, limited job prospects, and knowing they face a standard of living worse than their parents. Young workers face deteriorating wages and working conditions, as well as the ever-present threat of unemployment. Worries about health care, education, and other declining social services confront them at every step. The Covid-19 pandemic of 2020 has laid bare how starkly the profit system stands in contradiction to human needs.

The upsurge around racist police killings that shook the United States and the world in 2020 illustrated how millions are repelled by the horrors they see around them: never-ending imperialist wars; racism and police brutality; escalating attacks on women's rights; anti-immigrant scapegoating and violence; chauvinist hysteria; the growth of ultraright forces; the dehumanization and commodification of social relations. On top of all this, they see a looming catastrophe facing humanity due to the consequences of climate change and environmental destruction. All of these evils appear to them to have a common source: capitalism.

Despite this sentiment, however, relatively few of those now rallying to socialism know much about its history. Nor are most of them fully aware of the revolutionary thrust at the heart of socialism's legacy.

For this reason, an appreciation of the Second International—often referred to as the "Socialist International"—during the years its resolutions were guided by revolutionary Marxism is particularly relevant.[1]

An International Movement

A central tenet of the socialist movement for over 170 years has been internationalism.

"Workers of the world, unite!" has been socialism's slogan ever since Karl Marx and Frederick Engels issued this clarion call in the *Communist Manifesto*, published in 1848. Along these lines, the universal anthem of world socialism has been "The Internationale."

Putting that perspective into practice, Marx and Engels in 1864 helped organize and lead the International Workingmen's Association, better known as the First International. That association played a vital role in consolidating the emerging working-class movement around the world. It became known in particular for promoting the concept of international working-class solidarity, through the organization of support to strikes and other struggles by working people across borders. As Marx put it in 1872, "Let us bear in mind this fundamental principle of the International: solidarity! It is by establishing this life-giving principle on a reliable base among all the workers in all countries that we shall achieve the great aim which we pursue . . . the universal rule of the proletariat."[2]

Due to the primitive conditions of the early working-class movement, the First International had a short life span, declining precipitously after 1872 and formally dissolving in 1876. During the thirteen years that followed, various attempts were made to revive it. All were unsuccessful, however, coming up against the weakness of the organized proletarian movement in most countries. But by 1889, mass working-class parties and a growing trade union movement had begun to emerge. In this context, the world organization that became known as the Second International was founded.

The new movement—known at the time as Social Democracy—was formed under the direct guidance of Frederick Engels, who, after Marx's death in 1883, was the recognized leader of world socialism. Among the Second International's leading figures over the next twenty-five years were prominent left-wing socialists and Marxists: Eleanor Marx, August Bebel, Wilhelm Liebknecht, Paul Lafargue, Karl Kautsky, Jules Guesde, Rosa Luxemburg, Clara Zetkin, Georgy Plekhanov, Christian Rakovsky, and V. I. Lenin.

The role of Engels in the early years of the Second International is often not fully appreciated. Marx's lifelong collaborator played a central role in the Second International's founding in 1889, advising the organizers in detail on virtually all questions related to the political preparation and organization of the founding congress, along with helping to publicize the event. Engels subsequently played an important advisory role in the Second International's development up until his death in 1895.

A Heterogeneous Movement

From its beginning, the Second International was a loose association of widely divergent forces, with differing perspectives and expectations.

The movement included in its ranks both political parties and trade unions. A few of the political organizations were mass parties; others were small propaganda groups. Some of these forces had clearly defined Marxist programs; others still bore traits of pre-Marxist brands of socialism, with a multitude of conflicting perspectives, such as anarchism and syndicalism. The three largest contingents of the Second International were those in Germany, with a mass Social Democratic Party and large trade unions that looked to this party; Britain, with a number of relatively apolitical trade unions and a wide assortment of small political organizations; and France, with strong revolutionary traditions, but with the movement divided into opposing political currents.

The Second International's affiliates in different areas faced a wide variety of social and economic situations. Some countries, like Germany and Britain, were industrial powers with a well-developed proletariat. Other countries had primarily agrarian economies, with a large peasantry and a small working class. Some countries where socialists lived had ruling classes that possessed colonial empires; other peoples lived under the boot of colonialism and imperialism. State repression against socialist parties ranged from intermittent harassment to the imposition of total bans. As a result of all these differences, prevailing political cultures within the movement varied considerably.

Accomplishments and Strengths

In the quarter century of its existence, the Second International had a number of important accomplishments to its credit.

Perhaps its greatest achievement was to unify the international working-class movement under the banner of Marxism. And it helped disseminate and popularize the movement's strategic aim: the revolutionary overturn of the capitalist ruling class and its replacement by the rule of the proletariat, as a first step toward the establishment of socialism.

The founding congress in 1889 laid out the revolutionary goal of the new organization, affirming "that the emancipation of labor and humanity cannot occur without the international action of the proletariat—organized in class-based parties—which seizes political power through the expropriation of the capitalist class and the social appropriation of the means of production." (See page 22.)

The Second International of these years was, in its adopted resolutions, an irreconcilable revolutionary opponent of the capitalist system. While it championed the fight for reforms in the interests of working people—the eight-hour day, state-sponsored insurance and pensions, public education, votes for women, the right to asylum, and many other reform measures—it rejected the idea that capitalism as a system was reformable. It called for the working class to take political power and expropriate the capitalist owners of the major industries. It insisted that the working class itself was the agent of its own emancipation. And it defended the interests of all the oppressed and exploited around the world.

Two dates on the calendar today owe their existence to the Second International: May Day, established at the movement's founding congress in 1889 as a demonstration of working-class power and solidarity around the world; and International Women's Day, established in 1910 as a worldwide day of action for working women in the fight for full social and political rights.

The Second International showed the potential power of the organized working class. Camille Huysmans, the International Socialist Bureau's secretary, estimated that in the years before 1914 the Second International counted ten to twelve million members affiliated to its national sections, with over fifty million sympathizers and voters.[3] Numerous socialist representatives and deputies sat in national parliaments and regional and local legislative bodies.

For many workers, these signs of strength and seemingly uninterrupted growth gave them confidence that a revolutionary transformation of society was possible in the not-too-distant future.

Weaknesses and Contradictions

But behind this real and potential power were significant weaknesses and contradictions.

For one thing, the Second International was simply a loose federation of national parties and trade unions. The International possessed moral authority and made decisions on broad policy and strategy, to be put into practice by its affiliates. There was a positive side to this type of structure, particularly in the Second International's early years, as the movement consolidated itself politically.

But that structure came to be a serious weakness over time. No mechanism existed for implementation of the International's decisions, even after the 1900 creation of the International Socialist Bureau as the movement's executive body. Resolutions were often not put into practice. In the derisive words of the early Communist movement, the Second International functioned essentially as a "mailbox."[4] Such an appreciation was undoubtedly exaggerated and unfair, given that parties of the Second International regularly carried out important internationally coordinated actions during this period. It should be recognized, however, that these actions were generally organized on a party-to-party basis, without any real central control or coordination, even compared to that of the General Council of the First International decades earlier.[5]

Another weakness involved its geographic focus. Even though the Second International's reach extended to many countries, it was still predominantly a European and North American movement. While congress resolutions gave support to anticolonial struggles, most sections of the movement still had an underappreciation of those struggles. Moreover, the Second International never became a truly world movement. The only countries outside Europe, North America, and Australia that were ever represented at Second International congresses during the 1889–1912 period were Argentina, Japan, South Africa, and Turkish Armenia.

Similarly, the International's resolutions often lacked an adequate appreciation of the strategic allies the working class would need in its struggle—from toilers in the colonial world to working farmers and peasants, small shopkeepers, victims of national oppression, and others.

Finally, even though it called for the revolutionary replacement of capitalism, the Second International as a whole lacked a clear perspective on the role of revolutionary action in such a transformation. The relationship between reform and revolution was a constant point of friction and debate. An openly opportunist and reformist wing within its parties steadily grew.

Above all, the Second International was characterized by a gap between word and deed, as the day-to-day practice of most parties became increasingly dominated by a reformist and nonrevolutionary perspective. This gap and the growing divergences grew into a chasm in 1914 with the onset of the First World War. In clear violation of all the Second International's resolutions, the main parties of the Second International renounced their past pledges and lined up behind their governments' war efforts. Millions of workers and others were sent to their deaths, with the support of these parties.

In the words of Rosa Luxemburg, the Second International's leading representatives had thereby amended the *Communist Manifesto*'s call of "Workers of the world, unite," changing it to "Proletarians of all countries, unite in peacetime and cut each other's throats in wartime!"[6]

The betrayal of 1914 marked the political death of the Second International. Even though it was formally reconstituted in 1919, the new body lacked even the pretense of being a revolutionary movement. It consisted instead of open supporters of capitalist regimes and diehard opponents of the postwar revolutionary upsurge that developed in the wake of the Russian Revolution.

A Conflicted Legacy

Virtually all currents claiming to be socialist today formally acknowledge the Second International as part of their legacy. Yet, the Second International's resolutions during its Marxist period remain virtually unknown. Most are exceedingly difficult to even find. Astoundingly, the resolutions from its first nine congresses have never before been assembled together and published in their entirety in English.

What can be the explanation for this fact?

One obvious answer is that the Social Democratic parties of the post-1919 Second International were not interested in doing so. And for good reason.

Following the First World War and continuing over the next century, Social Democratic parties headed the government in a number of countries: Australia, Belgium, Britain, Finland, France, Germany, Sweden, Italy, Netherlands, Norway, Portugal, and others. They all defended capitalist rule both as parties in power and as loyal oppositions, and were willing participants or accomplices in numerous colonial and imperialist wars. It's not hard to understand why such parties would not want to be reminded of their revolutionary past. They would prefer to keep that chapter hidden and deeply buried.

But what about revolutionary socialists? Shouldn't they be interested in the resolutions of the Second International during its Marxist period?

The reality, however, is that most left-wing socialists and communists have had a conflicted view of the Second International's legacy.

In the years after the formation of the Third International—the Communist International (Comintern)—in 1919, many left-wing socialists wavered on whether to seek to rebuild the Second International or to construct an entirely new world movement. To these wavering elements, supporters of the Comintern repeatedly stressed the Second International's betrayal, and the need for a definitive break with it. Emphasis was placed on the need to turn one's back entirely on what had become a bankrupt organization that stood in the way of struggles by working people. Ever since then, generations of socialist activists have felt there was little value in studying the work or legacy of the Second International.

While that sentiment may be understandable, the conclusion is unwarranted. Downplaying the legacy of the Second International's Marxist period means cutting oneself off from an important part of the revolutionary movement's history, as well as the lessons to be learned from it. Doing so also means ceding that legacy to currents that sullied socialism's banner following 1914, and continue to do so. But the best of this legacy legitimately belongs to revolutionary-minded socialists and communists.

The revolutionary leaders who broke with the Second International after its betrayal of 1914, such as V. I. Lenin and Rosa Luxemburg, were not sparing in invective to label the betrayers. The vivid metaphor of the German Social Democratic Party as a "stinking corpse" is one of the more graphic descriptions.[7] What these revolutionaries criticized, above all, was the Second International's gap between word and deed, its hypocrisy.

In making these criticisms, however, Lenin and Luxemburg never renounced the resolutions the Second International had adopted. Quite the contrary. During the years of the First World War, for example, they constantly referred to the best of these resolutions—particularly the resolutions on militarism and war—to illustrate the extent to which the Second International's majority leaders were violating these resolutions in practice.

In addition to these programmatic points of continuity, the congresses of the Second International became places where the emerging revolutionary left wing began to collaborate and lay the foundations for their subsequent international efforts. At the 1907 congress, for example, Luxemburg and Lenin worked closely on the resolution on war and militarism. And at the 1910 congress, Lenin organized a small meeting of left-wing delegates to discuss areas of collaboration.

Debates in the Second International

Many of the resolutions adopted by the Second International, and printed in this book, were subjects of debate and controversy. Among these:

Debates with the anarchists. During the earlier years of the First International, there were heated exchanges with anarchists, a major current in the workers' movement at the time. Marx and Engels devoted considerable attention to this debate, above all with the anarchist leader Mikhail Bakunin. A central tenet of anarchist ideology was to reject all forms of political action, including participation in elections and the fight for political reforms and social legislation.

There were relatively few anarchists who participated as delegates in Second International congresses. But they once again raised objections to political action, making their presence known through regular disruptions of the proceedings. To prevent such disruptions, in 1891 a resolution on conditions of admission to the congress was adopted that called for recognition of political action as a precondition for attending international congresses, thereby excluding anarchists. Similar resolutions were approved in 1893 and in 1896, at which time anarchists were definitively placed outside the International.

Debates over the general strike and May Day. The question of the general strike was a point of contention at numerous congresses. This issue was generally put forward by delegates influenced by syndicalism, an ideology that tended to see unions as the essential instrument for revolutionary change. Many syndicalists viewed the general strike as the primary and surefire working-class weapon—above all, to combat the threat of war.

This overestimation of the potential of a general strike, however, was met by an opposite tendency to dismiss even the possibility of such a strike. Much of this opposition came from the German trade unions and their defenders in that country's Social Democratic Party. German unions were expanding rapidly at the time, along with a growing bureaucracy within them. Given the precarious legal situation then facing the working-class movement in Germany—even after the law banning socialist activity was lifted in 1890, restrictions on political and union activity remained—the German unions were afraid that such strikes could lead the government to outlaw them.

The overly cautious opposition to the general strike could also be seen on the question of May Day. In December 1888 the American Federation of Labor (AFL) voted to organize actions throughout the United States for the eight-hour day on May 1, 1890, in commemoration of the movement that began in the United States in 1886—a movement that had become known worldwide because of the Haymarket events that year in Chicago.[8]

The founding congress of the Second International in 1889 endorsed the AFL's initiative and voted to set May 1, 1890, as a day for demonstrations and strikes by working people around the world. From then on, May Day became a day to demonstrate the strength and solidarity of the international working-class movement.

Debates on May Day occurred at a number of congresses. The German and British trade unions and parties in particular were opposed to calling for strikes on May Day, preferring instead to schedule parades and rallies on the first Sunday in the month. Compromise resolutions were adopted at international congresses calling for strikes and demonstrations on May 1 where possible, but leaving the matter for ultimate decision by organizations in each country.

Debates over participation in capitalist governments and relations with bourgeois parties. At the congresses of Paris (1900) and Amsterdam (1904), debates centered on the question of socialist participation in capitalist governments and relations with bourgeois parties.

In 1899 French socialist Alexandre Millerand accepted a position as minister in the capitalist government of France. This move sparked a fierce controversy in the world socialist and working-class movement, given that socialists had always rejected accepting such posts. In the end, Second International resolutions condemned all participation by socialists in capitalist governments. Alongside that view, not giving support to bourgeois parties was seen by left-wing forces in the International as a principled question, in line with Karl Kautsky's assessment of "the bankruptcy of all capitalist parties."[9]

Debates over immigration. Heated debates occurred at the 1904 and 1907 congresses, as some socialists accepted anti-immigrant arguments that "backward," nonwhite workers could not be organized and took jobs away from native-born workers; as such, they endorsed the concept of restricting immigration. These racist arguments were sharply answered by those who supported the traditional socialist view opposing all immigration restrictions, a view that saw immigrants as fellow workers to be welcomed, championed, and organized into the working-class struggle.

Debates over colonialism. At the congresses of 1904 and 1907, the question of the new phenomenon of modern colonialism and imperialism was a hotly contested issue. A significant minority at these congresses supported the perspective of "socialist colonialism"—criticizing colonial abuses but supporting the idea of colonialism's "civilizing mission," and asserting that colonial rule and exploitation should still exist under socialism. The pro-colonialist position was ultimately rejected, but only by an astonishingly close vote.

Debates over trade unions. At several congresses, debates occurred over whether trade unions should be neutral on the question of working-class political power. Many conservative-minded trade union officials supported the idea that unions should focus exclusively on narrow, everyday issues such as wages and working conditions and not take up broad social and political questions. Coming out of these debates, the Second International reaffirmed the traditional Marxist view opposing the "neutrality" principle and stressing the need for permanent and close contact between trade unions and socialist parties.

The appendix to this book includes a number of unapproved resolutions that can help the reader see more clearly the issues in contention.

Through the debates around these and other issues, three distinct currents in the Second International crystallized in the years leading up to 1914: a large reformist and opportunist wing, a small but growing revolutionary left wing, and an amorphous centrist grouping that sought to straddle the other two sides, using Marxist language but increasingly adapting to opportunist forces.

Unevenness

By studying the Second International's adopted resolutions and motions in their entirety, their uneven nature is observable. Some resolutions are sharp and clear; others are ambiguous, vague, or contradictory. A tendency existed toward adopting compromise resolutions, in which conflicting views were sometimes papered over. Some of the adopted resolutions were drafted well prior to congresses, were circulated broadly, and received careful consideration. Other resolutions came about through delegates' motions on the congress floor that were approved with little or no discussion.

Despite this unevenness, the resolutions as a whole—with a few significant exceptions—were guided by the spirit of revolutionary Marxism. Most presented a clear socialist perspective on the major questions facing the working class and the oppressed, many of which remain acute today.

Contemporary Relevance

What is the value of these resolutions for new generations coming to socialism today?

Most of the major issues facing socialists at the present time are not new. Some have come up in different ways and contexts, but many of the issues in the fight today nevertheless bear a remarkable similarity to what they were over a century ago:

Political power. Probably the single biggest thread running through the resolutions adopted at Second International congresses was that every single major issue facing working people was inextricably tied to the question of political power, and the need to replace domination by capitalists and landlords with the rule of working people. In this spirit, it was generally assumed by the Second International that workers needed their own independent party, and that no political support was to be extended to the capitalist class or its parties. While the working class fights aggressively for reform measures, Second International resolutions stressed, the capitalist system as a whole was unreformable. A revolutionary transformation of the entire social order was necessary.

War and militarism. Workers need to oppose all imperialist wars, Second International resolutions asserted. Not an ounce of support should be extended to these ventures, they insisted. The old slogan of the German socialist movement "Not one penny, not one person" to the capitalist war machine guided the work of most socialists then and remains the stance socialists can look to now. The fight against militarism and war, together with the entire war machine, is a key task, part of the overall working-class struggle.

Imperialism and colonialism. Colonial conquest and plunder of the Third World was seen as simply an extension of capitalist exploitation, according to the Second International's adopted resolutions. Workers therefore need to actively support and champion the struggle for freedom by oppressed peoples fighting imperialist and colonialist domination, along with its racist justifications and rationalizations.

International solidarity. Numerous resolutions of the Second International centered on the international solidarity essential to the struggle of working people. Solidarity is a life-and-death question for the working class. Extending it is not an act of charity but rather an essential precondition for the success of workers' struggles.

Immigration. The Second International's resolution of 1907 pointed to the need to oppose all restrictions on the free immigration and emigration of workers, as well as to combat all forms of racist scapegoating. Immigrant workers should be viewed not as helpless victims but as welcome allies and reinforcements in the struggle against capitalism.

Democratic rights. Resolutions adopted at international congresses stressed the centrality of political and democratic rights. They viewed these rights as tools in the revolutionary struggle, and pointed to why the working class has the biggest stake in the fight to win them. Among the specific issues taken up in these resolutions are the fight against all antidemocratic restrictions, against political repression, for freedom of all political prisoners, for voting rights, for defense of the right to asylum, and for abolition of the death penalty.

Trade unions. The central importance of unions remains what it has been for over a century: as basic organizations to defend workers' interests. As Second International resolutions recognized, economics and politics are closely connected, which is why unions cannot be "neutral" in the political struggle. Strikes, boycotts, and other weapons in unions' arsenal need to be defended against all attempts to restrict the exercise of union power.

Labor legislation. The fight for laws limiting working hours, regulating working conditions, banning child labor, mandating equal pay for equal work, and guaranteeing workers the right to organize was central to socialists in the Second International. All of these issues remain of decisive importance for working people today.

Public education and cultural advancement. As socialists recognized over a century ago, public education as a right is a conquest of the working class in the fight to advance society. All attacks on this right need to be strongly combated. Access to education—including higher education—must be available to all, free of charge.

Women's emancipation. Under the impetus of female socialists like Clara Zetkin, multiple resolutions of the Second International addressed the oppression of women and how it is built into the very structure of capitalism. The fight against this oppression will play a central part in the overall revolutionary struggle, they pointed out. The struggle around this question today involves many decisive issues, including the fight for safe, legal, and accessible abortion; equal pay for equal work; free or low-cost child care; affirmative action; and elimination of all legal and social restrictions that prevent women from playing an equal role in society.

Who will bring about change? Resolutions of the Second International took it as a given that the working class itself is the agent of its own liberation. In the words of Karl Marx, incorporated into the founding rules of the First International, "The emancipation of the working classes must be conquered by the working classes themselves."[10] This same idea is at the heart of the rarely sung second verse of "The Internationale":

We want no condescending saviors
To rule us from a judgment hall;
We workers ask not for their favors;
Let us consult for all.
To make the thief disgorge his booty

To free the spirit from its cell,
We must ourselves decide our duty,
We must decide, and do it well.[11]

The long history of this fight for working-class self-emancipation extends back to the Revolutions of 1848, the Paris Commune of 1871, the Russian Revolution of 1917, the Cuban Revolution of 1959, and other revolutionary overturns around the world in which the working class entered onto the stage of history and sought to transform it—"storming the heavens," as Marx described working people during the Paris Commune.[12]

By linking up with the Second International's tradition and legacy—without overlooking its contradictions and weaknesses—those coming to the socialist movement today can take their place as part of this proud history.

About This Edition

This book is organized by congress. For each of the congresses, an introductory note is included that highlights the basic facts of the gathering and the key debates that took place there.

Within the chapters, resolutions are preceded by a short note that explains where the resolution came from, its author or presenter, and other relevant information. In this way, readers can judge for themselves the resolution's weight, importance, and character.

Many of the resolutions contain references to ones adopted at congresses. To assist the reader, references are provided throughout the book to the page number where these earlier resolutions can be found.

As noted previously, this volume is the first complete English-language collection of the resolutions adopted by the nine congresses of the Second International between 1889 and 1912.

French, German, and English were the three official languages of the Second International. The majority of its resolutions were thus prepared in all three languages. For this book the English-language versions that were prepared or published at the time have been utilized, where possible. These versions were how the resolutions came to be known among socialists in the English-speaking world.

Most resolutions and motions, however, were drafted in either French or German, and some of the original English translations were not particularly readable or even accurate. All the resolutions have therefore been edited for both content and readability, in consultation with the French and German versions.

Moreover, while official proceedings of the congresses were published in German (all nine) and French (six of them), only one congress had its proceedings published in English (1896). For this reason, a considerable number of the resolutions were not published at all in English and had to be translated for this volume in their entirety. For a listing of where each resolution came from, readers can consult the section on Sources for Resolutions.

In preparing this volume, the masterful bibliography of the Second International prepared by Georges Haupt was indispensable.[13] Another useful resource is the twenty-three volume *Histoire de la IIe Internationale*, published in Geneva by Minkoff Reprint.

Not included in this collection are the resolutions and motions adopted between congresses by the International Socialist Bureau—the Second International's executive body. While these resolutions are significant and deserve study, they nevertheless do not possess the authority of resolutions adopted by the congresses themselves.[14]

Three online archival collections have been especially valuable: the Second International Archives at the Internationaal Instituut voor Sociale Geschiedenis (International Institute of Social History, IISG); the Camille Huysmans Archive (Archief van Camille Huysmans) at AMSAB-ISG; and the Fonds Georges Haupt at Fondation Maison des sciences de l'homme (FMSH).[15]

A number of individuals have assisted in various aspects of the book. Among these, three deserve special mention: John Riddell, who provided general editorial collaboration, helped with translation, and contributed in numerous other ways; Bob Schwarz, who helped with research and editing; and Tom Alter, who made a number of useful editorial suggestions.

I also wish to acknowledge the help of John Barzman, Eric Blanc, Nisha Bolsey, Sebastian Budgen, Tineke Faber of the International Institute of Social History, Helen Ford at the University of Warwick Modern Records Centre, Daniel Gaido, Christine Gauvreau and Laura Katz Smith at the Connecticut State Library, Sophie Garrett at the University of Melbourne Archives, Leo Greenbaum of the Yivo Archives, Hershl Hartman, Peter Hudis, Sean Larson, Paul LeBlanc, Ben Lewis, Lars Lih, John McDonald, Myra Mniewski, Jean-Numa Ducange,

Nancy Rosenstock, Stephen R. Thornton, Gert Van Overstraeten of the Camille Huysmans Archive, and Lüko Willms. Any errors are the responsibility of the editor alone.

Mike Taber
August 2020

Resolutions of the Second International, 1889–1912

1.

Paris Congress, July 14–20, 1889

As the centennial year of the French Revolution, 1889 was the scene of a number of exhibitions and events in Paris. Among these were two important international congresses of working-class organizations.

At the time, French socialism was divided into opposing wings: a revolutionary Marxist current led by Jules Guesde and Paul Lafargue, and a reformist organization led by Paul Brousse. This latter tendency, whose overriding goal was to achieve reforms that it felt were possible under the capitalist system, came to be known as the "Possibilists."

Allied with the French Possibilists were the British Trades Union Congress and some other workers' organizations around the world. A November 1888 international conference initiated by the British unions voted to convene an international workers' congress in Paris in 1889, entrusting the organization of this to the French Possibilists. At about the same time, the Guesde-Lafargue party in France decided to convene a separate world congress of revolutionary-minded forces.

The prospect of two rival meetings at the same time and place was troubling to many in the workers' movement internationally. The leadership of the Social Democratic Party of Germany (SPD)—at the time the largest and most influential Marxist party in the world—invited both sides to attend a conference, held in The Hague on February 28, 1889, with the goal of uniting the two events. The Possibilists refused to attend, however. Instead, they went ahead on their own, issuing a call on March 11 for their congress. The Marxists responded by taking steps to convene a separate congress, sending out invitations to socialist parties, trade unions, and other workers' organizations.

One person deeply involved in helping to organize the Marxist gathering was Frederick Engels, the lifelong collaborator of Karl Marx. After Marx's death in 1883, he was considered by most socialists to be the most authoritative figure in the world movement. Engels grasped the significance of the proposed meeting, seeing its potential to revive the work of the of 1864–76 International Workingmen's Association—the First International, which Marx and he had helped lead.

In the months leading up to the congress, Engels maintained a voluminous correspondence with the leaders of the international socialist movement. His letters on the preparations and organization of this congress would fill a small volume.[1] He also did what he could to publicize the event.

One concern of Engels was that the organizers might be so eager to unify the two competing congresses that they would conciliate with the Possibilists on programmatic questions, watering down the movement's revolutionary principles and thereby bringing unclarity into the world socialist movement. While not opposed in principle to a united congress, Engels was convinced that only one based around a clear socialist program and perspective could provide a lasting basis for effective international working-class organization and action.

On July 14, 1889 (the centenary of Bastille Day), the two congresses convened separately in Paris, attended by delegates from socialist parties and trade unions. The gatherings were roughly comparable in size: the Marxist congress drew 408 delegates from 24 countries; the Possibilist event was attended by 567 delegates from 14 countries.

Many prominent world socialist leaders were present at the Marxist congress: Wilhelm Liebknecht, August Bebel, Eduard Bernstein, and Clara Zetkin from Germany; Jules Guesde, Édouard Vaillant, and Paul Lafargue from France; Eleanor Marx, William Morris, and Keir Hardie from Britain; Victor Adler from Austria; Georgy Plekhanov from Russia; Ferdinand Domela Nieuwenhuis from the Netherlands. Several delegates had been participants in the First International, such as César de Paepe and Leo Frankel. A number were veterans of the Paris Commune of 1871.

As Engels had foreseen, it was the Marxist congress, with its programmatic clarity and broader representation, that won the day. Even while both congresses were still in session, a few delegates from the Possibilist gathering started drifting into the Marxist event. Within a relatively short time, the Possibilist congress was largely forgotten, relegated to the status of a historical footnote. The Marxist congress, on the other hand, was the first meeting of what would become known as the Second International.

One of the resolutions of the 1889 congress was to have an especially important and lasting impact on the international working-class movement: the decision to embrace the initiative of the American Federation of Labor in calling for an internationally coordinated day of action on behalf of the eight-hour day. That initiative was meant to commemorate the movement begun in the United States in 1886—a struggle that became known worldwide because of the Haymarket events that year in Chicago.[2] With this in mind, May 1, 1890, was set as a day of demonstrations and strikes around the world to fight for the eight-hour-day demand. May Day has since become institutionalized as an international workers' holiday—a day for demonstrating the power of the labor movement around the world.

Giving a balance sheet of the Paris Congress, Engels wrote that it proved to be "a brilliant success."[3]

UNITY OF THE SOCIALIST MOVEMENT
AND INTERNATIONAL CONGRESSES

Resolution presented by Wilhelm Liebknecht. The subject concerns the continued efforts toward unification with the Possibilist congress that was meeting in Paris at the same time.

The Congress notes that participants in the Hague conference and the Paris organizational committee have expressed their sincere desire for an agreement among all socialist parties and workers' organizations with respect to the International Congress, and regrets that the steps taken to this end have not led to achievement of this goal.[4]

The Congress affirms that unity is the indispensable precondition for liberation of the proletariat. Every Social Democrat is therefore duty-bound to leave no stone unturned in taking measures to overcome discord.

The Congress therefore declares that it still stands ready to come to an understanding for unity, provided that the forces taking part in the other congress adopt a resolution along these lines that is acceptable to all participants in our Congress.

* * *

INTERNATIONAL LABOR LEGISLATION

Resolution based on drafts by August Bebel and Jules Guesde.

The International Socialist Labor Congress of Paris:

Having affirmed that the emancipation of labor and humanity cannot occur without the international action of the proletariat—organized in class-based parties—which seizes political power through the expropriation of the capitalist class and the social appropriation of the means of production;

Considering:

That the rapid development of capitalist production has been imposed on all countries, one after the other;

That the advance of capitalist production implies the increasing exploitation of the working class by the bourgeoisie;

That this increasingly intensive exploitation results in the political oppression of the working class, its economic subjugation, and its physical and moral degeneration;

That it is therefore the duty of workers of all countries to struggle, by all means at their disposal, against this social structure that weighs down on them and simultaneously threatens the free development of humanity. Above all, the task is to oppose the destructive actions of the present economic order.

The Congress resolves:

Effective protective legislation is an absolute necessity in all countries where capitalist production prevails.

As the basis of this legislation, the Congress calls for:

(a) Limiting the workday to a maximum of eight hours for adults.

(b) Ending labor for children under fourteen years of age; from fourteen to eighteen, the workday to be reduced to six hours for both sexes.

(c) Eliminating night work, except for certain branches of industry that by their nature require uninterrupted functioning.

(d) Ending labor for women in all branches of industry that are especially harmful to women's bodies.

(e) Eliminating night work for women and workers under the age of eighteen.

(f) Uninterrupted rest of at least thirty-six hours a week for all workers.

(g) Ending certain types of industry and certain methods of manufacturing that are prejudicial to the health of workers.

(h) Ending the system of subcontracting.

(i) Eliminating payment in kind.

(j) Eliminating hiring intermediaries.

(k) Monitoring of all workshops and industrial establishments, including domestic industry, by inspectors paid by the state, at least half of whom are to be elected by the workers themselves.

The Congress declares that all these measures of public health must be defined by law and international treaties, which proletarians of all countries are urged to impose on their governments. The application of these laws and treaties, obtained in the manner deemed most effective, must be subject to monitoring and supervision.

The Congress declares, further, that it is the duty of workers to admit women into their ranks, on the basis of equality, and on the principles of equal work and equal pay for workers of both sexes and irrespective of nationality.

For this reason, as well as for the complete emancipation of the proletariat, the Congress considers it essential to organize workers in all fields, and consequently to demand absolute freedom of association and coalition.

* * *

WAYS AND MEANS FOR WINNING DEMANDS

The International Socialist Labor Congress of Paris:

Urges workers' organizations and socialist parties of all countries to immediately set themselves to work, using all means (meetings, journals, petitions, demonstrations, etc.) to lead their respective governments:

1. To adhere to the intergovernmental conference of Bern, proposed by the Swiss government.[5]

2. To support at that congress the resolutions of the Paris International Congress.

In all countries with socialist elected representatives, these should bring the resolutions of the Paris Congress into municipal councils and parliaments.

In all elections, both municipal and legislative, these same resolutions should be part of the program of socialist candidates.

An executive commission is hereby created for the Paris Congress resolutions, with regard to the international labor legislation projected by the Swiss republic.

This commission, composed of five members, is charged with directly transmitting to the Bern conference the key demands that the labor organizations and socialist parties of Europe and America, meeting in Paris July 14–20, view as indispensable elements of international labor protection.

This commission is also given authority to convene the next international congress, which shall be held in a locality of Switzerland or Belgium, to be designated later.

Under the title *La Journée de huit heures* [the eight-hour day], a newspaper will be published, with the help of socialist parties represented at the Paris International Congress. The goal of this weekly organ is to centralize all information about the various national movements aimed at legislation to reduce the workday.[6]

* * *

INTERNATIONAL DEMONSTRATION ON MAY 1, 1890

Motion presented by Raymond Lavigne, as amended by the congress.

The Congress resolves that a great international demonstration shall be organized in such a manner that on a fixed day the workers in all countries and in all cities shall simultaneously present to the public powers the demand that the duration of the working day be set at eight hours, and that the other resolutions of the International Congress at Paris be enacted into law.

In view of the fact that the holding of such a demonstration on May 1, 1890, has already been resolved by the American Federation of Labor at its congress of December 1888 in St. Louis, this date is herewith fixed as the day for the international demonstration.[7]

The workers of the various nations shall organize such a demonstration in a manner best suited to the conditions in their country.

* * *

ABOLITION OF STANDING ARMIES / GENERAL ARMING OF THE POPULATION

Resolution originally drafted by Édouard Vaillant.

The International Socialist Labor Congress of Paris,
    Considering:
    That the standing army or the armed force in the service of the ruling or possessing class is the negation of all democratic or republican rule, the military expression of the monarchic or oligarchic and capitalist regime, and an instrument of reactionary coup d'états and social oppression;
    That the standing army, and the offensive policy of which it is the organ, is the result and cause of the system of aggressive wars and poses a constant danger of international conflicts. This system must give way

to the defensive and peaceful policy of democracy, to the organization of the whole nation drilled and armed, not for pillage and conquest, but to safeguard its independence and its liberty;

That the standing army, incessant cause of war, is, as history proves, incapable of defending a country against the superior forces of a coalition. Its defeat leaves the country disarmed, at the mercy of the conquerors, while a nation prepared, organized, and armed would be inaccessible to invasion;

That a standing army is the disorganization of all civil life, taking from every nation the flower of its youth in order to shut it in barracks, demoralize it, at the period of apprenticeship, study, greater activity, and action;

That work, science, and art are thus sterilized and stunted; the very existence and development of the citizen, the individual, and the family are harmed;

That on the other hand, in a really national army, or armed nation, the citizen follows the development of his aptitudes, his faculties in the national life; he executes his military duties as a necessary attribute of his capacity as a citizen;

Considering that:

The standing army, by the cost of the continuously accrued war debt, by the ever-increasing taxes and loans that it brings about, is a cause of misery and ruin;

The Congress:

Resolutely repudiates the bellicose proposals entertained by the governments for evil ends;

Declares that peace as a primary condition is indispensable to all labor emancipation;

And demands, with the abolition of standing armies, the general arming of the people on the following lines:

The national army or the armed nation formed of all available citizens, organized by district in such a way that each town, each canton, has its own battalion, composed of citizens who know each other, assembled, armed, equipped and ready to march, if necessary, in twenty-four hours. Each one shall keep his own rifle and equipment, as in Switzerland, for the defense of public liberty and national security.

Moreover, the Congress declares that war, fatal outcome of the present economic conditions, will disappear entirely only with the disappearance of the capitalist order, with the emancipation of labor, and the international triumph of socialism.

* * *

POLITICAL AND ECONOMIC ACTION

Presented by J. F. Busche, delegate of the US Socialist Labor Party, and L. E. Miller, delegate of the Jewish Federation of Trade Unions of New York.

Whereas the reports of the delegates of all countries to this Congress have shown that the organization of labor (trade unions and similar groups) is in itself insufficient for obtaining the emancipation of the working class, while agitation to reduce the workday, limit the labor of women and children, and establish protective labor laws has demonstrated its capacity to develop class consciousness among workers, a necessary preliminary for the self-emancipation of the working class;

Whereas the history of the workers' movement shows that appeals by the workers to the bourgeoisie have no effect, and only work to the political advantage of the ruling class;

Whereas the possession of political power by the ruling class allows it to maintain its exploitative system of private ownership and capitalist production;

Whereas this political power blocks the control of industry by the state, and the control of the state by the people;

The Paris International Congress resolves:

1. That in all the countries where proletarians possess the vote, they should join the ranks of the Socialist Party. They should tolerate no compromise with any other political party, and through the use of the ballot and under the authority of their respective constitution, obtain the conquest of political power.

2. That within all countries in which proletarians are denied the electoral franchise and constitutional rights, they should struggle by all possible means to obtain the right to vote.

3. That every use of repressive force on the part of the ruling class to hinder the peaceful evolution of society toward cooperative organization, both industrial and social, would be a crime against humanity. Such inhumanity would subject the aggressors to punishment carried out by those who fight for the defense of their life and their liberty.

2.

Brussels Congress, August 16–22, 1891

Attended by 337 delegates from sixteen countries, the Brussels Congress of the Second International effectively healed the breach between the two rival congresses held two years earlier. The main reformist forces that had attended the Possibilist gathering of 1889 were participants at Brussels.

Also present and highly visible at the congress were several anarchist delegates. At the time, anarchism was a major current in the workers' movement. A central tenet of anarchists was to reject all forms of political action, including participation in elections and the fight for political reforms and social legislation. At several points during the congress, anarchist delegates engaged in noisy and disruptive procedural protests, harkening back to anarchists' participation in the First International, which had led to a split in 1872. With this experience in mind, the Brussels Congress adopted a motion excluding anarchist organizations from participating in the congress in their own name.

Other points of contention at the congress involved the general strike and militarism, as well as the call for international actions on the First of May.

Frederick Engels made his assessment of the Brussels Congress in a letter to Friedrich Adolph Sorge, who had been a fellow leader of the First International decades earlier. "In matters of principle as of tactics the Marxists have been victorious all along the line," Engels wrote. A few days later, he added, "The Congress has proved a brilliant success for us. . . . The new, incomparably larger and avowedly Marxist International is beginning again at the precise spot where its predecessor [the First International] left off."[1]

CONDITIONS OF ADMISSION TO THE CONGRESS

Remarks by Jean Volders presenting a motion on behalf of the Belgian delegation on anarchist participation in the congress. After extensive discussion, the congress voted overwhelmingly to reject the credentials of the Belgian anarchist delegate whom Volders refers to.

Belgium is represented by 187 delegates from political and trade union organizations. However, one case requires clarification. Three anarchist delegates are present. As anarchists, they have no business attending a *socialist* congress. Two of them, however, have come as delegates of nonanarchist groups. That leaves in question the mandate of only a single delegate. The Belgian Workers Party requests that this delegate be excluded on the grounds that anarchists support neither organization of the workers [in unions] nor legislative initiatives by governments in the workers' interests. There is therefore no basis for their participation in this congress.

***

LABOR LEGISLATION

Commission resolution presented by Émile Vandervelde, incorporating amendments by Leo Frankel and British trade unionists. In the discussion on this resolution, German SPD leader August Bebel sought to put the question of labor legislation in a revolutionary perspective: "I wish above all to emphasize that in my opinion the chief task of Social Democracy is not to secure laws for labor protection, but to explain to the workers the nature and character of present-day society, in order that this society should disappear as quickly as possible, the more quickly as it bears within itself, by virtue of its own laws of development, the fatal germ of its own decay. The workers must learn to understand the nature of this society so that when its last hour has struck, they will be able to establish the new society."[2]

This Congress, recognizing the existence of the class struggle and convinced that as long as class rule prevails the emancipation of the working classes will be impossible, declares that the laws enacted and the decrees issued in various countries since the Paris International Congress held in 1889 do not in any respect meet the aspirations of the workers. That although the Berlin conference [on labor legislation], as admitted by those who themselves initiated it, met under the pressure exerted by the International Labor Congress and may therefore be regarded as an important concession to public opinion, the results have demonstrated that existing governments do not wish to effect necessary reforms, and that, on the other hand, the resolutions of the Berlin conference have been used as a pretext by certain manufacturing countries to arrest the development of protective labor legislation by invoking the decisions of the Berlin conference and pointing to the defects in the legislation of competing countries.[3] Moreover, this Congress affirms that in cases in which legislation is not defective, its application is allowed to remain inoperative.

For these reasons, this Congress urges upon the workers of all countries to agitate for the realization of the program laid down by the Paris Congress, if only to make it clear to the workers that the governing and exploiting classes are hostile to legislation effectively protecting the interests of labor.

Whereas it is necessary to give to the international labor movement a common impulse, especially in the direction of protective labor legislation, therefore be it resolved by this Congress:

1. To organize in every country a permanent commission of inquiry concerning the conditions of labor in its relation to working-class legislation.

2. To collect, collate, and exchange all necessary information with a view to the development and unification of all the said legislation.

3. This Congress recommends that the wageworkers of the whole world unite their efforts against the domination of capital, and, wherever they enjoy political rights, to exercise them with the object of gaining their emancipation from the wages system.

* * *

WORKING-CLASS ORGANIZATION AND ACTION

Commission resolution as amended by the congress.

Under the present economic conditions, and with the unceasing efforts of the ruling classes to suppress more and more the political rights of the working classes, and to reduce their economic standard of living, strikes as well as boycotts are to be considered as an unavoidable means to be used by the laboring classes for the purpose of resisting the attempts of their adversaries to encroach on their political rights and make their material life one of misery and unendurable privations. They are to be considered at the same time as a means to better as far as possible their political and social position within the now-existing society.

But whereas strikes and boycotts are double-edged weapons which, when used at an unfavorable time and in the wrong place may do more harm than good, this Congress recommends a careful investigation of all the circumstances that should be taken into consideration, before these arms are taken up with any hope of success.

And furthermore this Congress considers it necessary before entering into any fights of this kind, to organize trade unions, so that they are enabled to gain their purposes by the weight of their numbers, as well as by their financial means.

Therefore:

The Congress recommends all workers to support with all their strength trade union organizations, and protests against all attempts on the part of governments or owners to interfere in any fashion whatever with the right of coalition of the workers.

In order to ensure this right of coalition, the Congress demands the repeal of all laws that either directly or indirectly attack this right, and declares it to be the duty of the workers to pursue this end with all their strength.

And since, desirable as it is, a central organization of the international forces of the workers for the moment presents difficulties of various kinds, the Congress decides to provide a common means for the working-class solidarity of the different countries to manifest itself.

And therefore recommends wherever it is possible the formation in every country of a national correspondence committee (*secrétariat du travail*) in order that, when a struggle breaks out anywhere between capital and labor, the workers of the different nationalities may be informed of the circumstances and be in a position to act accordingly.

* * *

PIECEWORK

Resolution presented by Louis Bertrand from Belgium.

Considering:

That piecework and contract work is becoming more and more generalized;

That this form of wages constantly intensifies the exploitation of the labor force, and consequently increases the poverty and misery of the workers;

That it reduces more and more the worker to the status of a machine;

That it decreases the rate of wages as a result of fierce competition among workers, in which the productivity of an elite group of workers is set as a standard;

That this system is a perpetual cause of conflict between bosses and workers, and among workers themselves;

That, finally, it tends to generalize homework in place of factory work within a great number of trades, as well as undermining the spirit of association, preventing workers from organizing, and rendering impossible the application of protective labor laws;

The Congress considers that this abominable system of overwork is a necessary consequence of the capitalist system and will disappear along with it.

It is the duty of workers' organizations of all countries to oppose by every means the development of this system.

The sweating system [sweatshops], too, leads to disastrous consequences and must be fought for the same reasons.

* * *

INTERNATIONAL FIRST OF MAY DEMONSTRATIONS

Motion proposed by the French delegation, as amended by the congress. In the commission that discussed this resolution, the German and British delegations expressed opposition to calling for a cessation of work on May 1, and proposed instead that demonstrations be held the first Sunday in the month. The following is the compromise resolution adopted.

The Congress,

In order to maintain the true economic character of the First of May, viz., the demand for a legal eight-hour working day and the affirmation of the class struggle;

The Congress decides:

That there shall be one common demonstration for this purpose by the workers in all countries;

That this demonstration shall be the First of May, where possible, and that all shall cease work on that day.

* * *

WOMEN'S EQUALITY

Adopted by the congress on a motion by Wilhelmina Drucker, Emma Ihrer, Louise Kautsky, Anna Kuliscioff, and Ottilie Baader.

The Congress invites the socialist parties and labor parties of all countries to affirm energetically in their programs the complete equality of the two sexes and to demand that women be granted the same political and civil rights as men, and the repeal of all laws placing women outside public rights.

* * *

THE JEWISH QUESTION

Abraham Cahan, a delegate from the United Hebrew Trades in the United States, had made an appeal to the congress to address the Jewish question and anti-Semitism. Responding on behalf of a commission that took up this question, Belgian socialist Jean Volders condemned anti-Semitic agitation as a capitalist device to sow division among the working class. But Volders stated that the congress need do nothing more than make a general statement to this effect, declaring that it recognized no distinction of race or nationality, and linking condemnation of anti-Semitism with that of "philo-Semitism." A resolution on anti-Semitism adopted by the 1904 Amsterdam Congress presented an entirely different perspective on the question (see pages 92–93). The Brussels Congress commission's resolution, below, was adopted unanimously.

The Congress:

Considering that socialist and labor parties of all countries have always affirmed that for them racial or national antagonism and struggle cannot exist, but only the class struggle of proletarians of all races against capitalists of all races;

Considering that for the Jewish-language working-class population, there can be no other means of emancipation than through unity with the labor or socialist parties of their respective countries;

While condemning both anti-Semitic and philo-Semitic agitation as one of the maneuvers by which the capitalist class and reactionary governments seek to divert the socialist movement and divide workers;

Decides that there is no need to take up the question proposed by the delegation of American Jewish-language socialist groups, and passes to the next order of business.

* * *

MILITARISM

Commission resolution, prepared by Wilhelm Liebknecht and Édouard Vaillant. A counterresolution presented by Ferdinand Domela Nieuwenhuis for the Dutch delegation called for a general strike against the threat of war; that resolution was rejected. For the text of the Dutch resolution, see the appendix, page 149.

The Congress:

Declares that militarism, which bears down heavily on Europe, is the fatal result of the permanent state of open and latent war, imposed on society by the system of the exploitation of man by man and the class struggle that is the consequence of this.

Declares that all attempts to obtain the abolition of militarism and the establishment of peace among the nations—however generous be their intentions—can only be utopian and powerless if they do not touch the economic sources of the evil.

Declares that only the creation of a socialist order, putting an end to the exploitation of man by man, will put an end to militarism and assure permanent peace.

Declares that consequently it is the duty of all those who wish to finish with war to join the international socialist party, which is the true and only party of peace.

Therefore the Congress:

In view of the situation in Europe that daily becomes more threatening, and of the chauvinist inciting of the governing classes in the various countries, calls on all workers to protest, by means of unceasing agitation, against all desires for war and against the alliances that favor such, and to hasten, by the development of the international organization of the proletariat, the triumph of socialism.

Declares that it is the only means capable of averting a general war, the expenses of which all workers would have to bear.

In any case, the Congress intends, in the presence of history and humanity, to throw all responsibility for whatever happens onto the ruling classes.

* * *

MOTION ON MARITIME WORKERS

Motion by Raymond Lavigne, delegate from Bordeaux.

The Congress urges all labor parties of the world to support the organization of seafaring workers, as well as to publicize the international maritime congress that will take place in Bordeaux in 1892.[4]

3.

Zurich Congress, August 6–12, 1893

The Second International's Zurich Congress of 1893 drew 439 delegates from twenty countries.

Noteworthy among those attending was an official delegation from the British trade unions, which gave the congress added international authority.

As with the 1891 Brussels Congress, anarchists played a disruptive role in Zurich. Consequently, a motion was adopted that the congress be open to all those who recognized the need for working-class political action. Since the anarchists rejected such action, the motion effectively excluded them from the congress.

Debates on the idea of a general strike against war and on the question of May Day, which had arisen at the 1891 Brussels Congress, came up again in Zurich.

A highlight of the congress was the closing address given by seventy-two-year-old Frederick Engels, who was elected honorary president of the final session. "We must continue to work on common ground," Engels told the delegates. "We must permit discussion in order not to become a sect, but the common standpoint must be retained. The loose association, the voluntary bond which is furthered by congresses, is sufficient to win us the victory which no power in the world can snatch from us again."[1]

CONDITIONS OF ADMISSION TO THE CONGRESS

The point of this resolution was to exclude the anarchists, who did not rec-ognize the need for political action. The first paragraph was moved by Paul Argyriadès, A. Bonnet, J. Mojonnet, Auguste Keufer, Saint-Domingue, Edmond Degay, Eugène Guérard, B. Mortier, Victor Renou, Louis Fière, Léon Rémy, Marchand, and Marianne. The second paragraph was pro-posed by Victor Adler, B. Edwards, August Bebel, Karl Kautsky, Wilhelm Liebknecht, Marya Jankowska-Mendelson, and Otto Lang.

All trade unions shall be admitted to the Congress; also those socialist parties and organizations that recognize the necessity of the organiza-tion of the workers and of political action.

By "political action" is meant that the working-class organizations seek, as far as possible, to use or conquer political rights and the ma-chinery of legislation for the furthering of the interests of the proletariat and the conquest of political power.

* * *

THE EIGHT-HOUR DAY

Commission resolution, as amended by the congress.

The Congress resolves:

The eight-hour day is one of the most important preconditions for the definitive liberation of the working class from the yoke of capital. It is also the most important available measure to improve their conditions of life.

The eight-hour day reduces unemployment, increases workers' pro-ductivity, raises their pay, and enlarges their purchasing capacity.

The eight-hour day enhances family life, which is disrupted by the capitalist system, and makes it possible to improve child welfare.

The eight-hour day improves the people's health, strength, intelli-gence, and morality.

The eight-hour day provides the working class with increased time for trade-union and political activity. Only then are political rights and freedoms rendered effective and useful as tools for workers' social liberation.

The campaign for the eight-hour day must be waged in every country, since this is the only way to secure its introduction and its manifold benefits.

The Congress proposes the following measures to win the eight-hour day on an international level:

• Organization of the working class in both trade unions and political parties and their utilization to carry out both agitation and propaganda for the eight-hour day.

• Agitation for the eight-hour day should be carried out through leaflets, lectures, the socialist press, demonstrations, and rallies; and in political institutions of every sort, in national, regional, and municipal assemblies. The socialist press should feature an ongoing column titled "The Eight Hour Day," which reports on all events and efforts to this end. Workers' representatives in political assemblies should propose from time to time measures to shorten the hours of work, particularly for workers employed in the public service.

• Socialist representatives in national parliaments should come to agreement on a common legal proposal to introduce the eight-hour day on an international level, and should press the governments of all industrialized countries to join in an international conference to introduce it.

• The trade unions should wage an independent struggle with the bosses, outside the political arena, for introduction of the eight-hour day and, in this way, prepare the ground to win this measure for the working class as a whole.

* * *

POLITICAL ACTION

Commission resolution presented to the congress by Émile Vandervelde.

I

The Congress declares that political action is only a means of achieving the economic emancipation of the proletariat, referring to the decisions of the Brussels Congress on the class struggle [see pages 31–32]:

1. That it is necessary for workers of all countries to organize nationally and internationally into labor unions and other organizations for struggling against their exploiters.

2. That political action is necessary not only from the point of view of agitation and of the affirmation of socialist principles as a whole, but also from the point of view of the realization of reforms of immediate interest. Consequently, we recommend to the workers of all countries to conquer political rights, and to make use of them in all legislative and administrative bodies, for the purpose of realizing the demands of the proletariat, and to gain possession of political power, which is today only an instrument of capitalist domination, in order to transform it into a means for the emancipation of the proletariat.

3. That the form of political and economic struggle must be determined according to circumstances by the various nationalities. But in all cases the revolutionary aim of the socialist movement must be made fundamental: namely, the complete transformation of present society from the economic, moral, and political points of view. In no case can political action be used for compromise or for alliances that would contradict the principles and the independence of socialist parties.

II

Whereas the forms of representation in present-day society do not accurately reflect the thoughts and desires of those who are represented;

And whereas the prevailing constituency system in most countries is set up for election by majority;

These conditions can only increase the conflict between the will of the people and the votes of its representatives.

The Congress therefore advocates the achievement of complete popular sovereignty through proportional representation and also through the right to propose and approve laws (initiative and referendum).

* * *

THE AGRARIAN QUESTION

Commission resolution presented to the congress by Charles Victor Jaclard.

The Congress affirms the right of the community to the soil above and below.

The Congress declares that one of the most pressing duties of the Social Democracy of all countries is to organize the agricultural laborers no less than the industrial workers, and to incorporate them into the ranks of the army of international socialism.

The Congress decides that all nationalities shall present to the next congress a report on the progress of the propaganda in the rural districts, and on the agrarian situation generally in their respective countries.

These reports shall especially indicate what attitude, what means, what method of propaganda the socialists of these respective countries consider as best suited to their own agrarian situation as regards the different categories of agricultural laborers, such as small peasants, proprietors, métayers [sharecroppers], etc.

The Congress, in view of the capital importance of the land question and the insufficient attention it has hitherto received at international congresses, recommends that it be placed first on the agenda at the next congress.

* * *

NATIONAL AND INTERNATIONAL ORGANIZATION OF TRADE UNIONS

Commission resolution presented by Adolph von Elm. It was adopted by the congress incorporating an amendment by Jean Volders.

Referring to the resolution on strikes and boycotts voted at the Brussels Congress of 1891 [see pages 31–32] and in accordance with it, the International Congress of Zurich 1893 resolves:

Making the struggle of the working classes in the domain of economics into a centralized and effective one is possible only by the organization of the workers. It is the duty of all workers conscious of their class to join their respective organizations. It is the duty of the political workers' party and of the workers' newspapers to advance the trade organizations of the workers with all their energy. The trade unions are destined to be the pillars of the organization of the coming society and therefore the further strengthening of them is, alongside the conquering of political power, an absolute necessity.

The united efforts of the capitalists to reduce the standard of living of the workers necessitate a stronger union than ever between the forces of trade unionism, to cultivate a community of interest of all workers in all industries and all countries, notwithstanding all differences of race and religion, and an active mutual support in all their struggles against capitalism.

I

For this purpose the Congress recommends:

1. The formation of national unions of the different trades.

2. International arrangements for mutual support.

3. The establishment of national workers' bureaus, where all federations are to be represented. It is their duty to exchange all information of importance about the labor movement, strikes and lockouts, and the annual reports of the different trade societies.

4. In order to bring about a centralized organization of the information as to the labor market, trade societies [unions] shall demand everywhere of the municipalities the establishment of labor exchanges, the management of which shall be conferred only upon the trade societies of the place.

II

As regards more especially America and Australia:

Whereas the development of capitalism in those great countries has reached a point where the purely economic organization of their wageworkers must soon become absolutely powerless unless it be supplemented by independent political action on the lines of the international socialist movement; and

Whereas their growing importance in the economy of the world and the cosmopolitan character of their populations is raising vital questions concerning the conditions of existence of the European proletariat and the progress of the social revolution;

Be it resolved that the Congress urges upon the trade unions of America and Australia not only the benefit of entering as soon as possible into direct relations with the corresponding trade unions and labor syndicates of Europe upon the plan above proposed, but also and above all the necessity of repudiating the bourgeois political parties that betray and oppress them, and of constituting themselves into great socialist labor parties, marching with their European brethren to the emancipation of the working classes.

III

The Italian delegates, aware of the baneful influence exercised by the immigration and competition of unorganized foreign workers on the labor and socialist organizations of several countries, invite the socialist and labor organizations of those countries affected by such "disloyal competition" to extend the social propaganda and the spirit of resistance among the workers of foreign nationalities. The Italian delegates promise on their part the cooperation of the Italian socialists in the matter. They will furnish reports on Italian emigration, will enlighten the toilers of their country, and will circulate socialist and labor literature among the Italian workers abroad.

Viewing the question from a general point of view, the Congress resolves:

That it is advisable for the socialist and labor organizations of all nations where the evil effects of the competition brought about by the immigration of foreign unorganized labor are mostly felt, to extend among the latter the organization and the propagation of the principles of international solidarity.

That the socialist and labor organizations requiring information or aid should address themselves through their general national secretaries to the central representatives of similar bodies in the countries from which the immigration comes.

* * *

COMMON ACTION WITH REGARD TO
FIRST OF MAY DEMONSTRATION

Commission resolution presented by Jean Volders, as amended by the congress.

The Congress reaffirms the resolution of the Brussels Congress [see pages 33–34] as follows:

In order to secure for the First of May its specially economic character, the demand for the eight-hour day, and the proclamation of the class war;

The Congress decides:

The First of May is a general holiday on which the workers of all nations shall demonstrate the solidarity of their interests and their demands.

This holiday shall be a day of rest from work, as far as this is not rendered impossible by the circumstances of the respective countries.

The Congress resolves furthermore the following addition:

It is the duty of the Social Democracy of every country to strive for a celebration of the First of May as a *day of rest from work*, and to support the local organizations in their endeavors in that direction.

It is further resolved:

The First of May demonstration for obtaining the eight-hour day shall at the same time be the manifestation of a firm resolve on the part of the working classes to destroy all forms of class distinctions, as the only way that leads to the peace of the peoples and to peace and good will between the nations of the world.

* * *

PROTECTIVE LEGISLATION FOR WORKING WOMEN

Commission resolution presented by Louise Kautsky, as amended by the congress.

Considering:

That the bourgeois women's rights movement rejects all special legislation on behalf of working women as an attack upon the freedom of women and upon her equal rights as opposed to men;

That thus it, on the one hand, leaves out of account the conditions of our modern society, a society based upon the exploitation of the working class—women and men—by the capitalist class;

That on the other hand, it does not take into account the special and peculiar function of women, a function imposed upon her by the differentiation of sex, a function of such tremendous importance for the future of society—that of the mother of children;

The International Socialist Workers Congress of Zurich declares:

It is the duty of the labor representatives in all countries to insist upon protective legislation for women by securing the following measures:

1. A maximum working day of eight hours for women, and of six hours for young persons under eighteen.

2. Cession of work for thirty-six consecutive hours in every week.

3. Prohibition of night labor.

4. Prohibition of labor in all trades especially dangerous to health.

5. Prohibition of women working two weeks before, and four weeks after, confinement [for childbirth].

6. The appointment of an adequate number of women inspectors for all trades and industries in which women are employed.

7. The above provisions to apply to all girls and women employed in factories, workshops, shops, home industries, and in agricultural labor.

* * *

SOCIAL DEMOCRACY IN THE EVENT OF WAR

Commission resolution presented by Georgy Plekhanov, proposed originally by the German delegation. The Dutch delegation submitted a resolution similar to the one it had proposed in 1891 calling for an international general strike against war (see the appendix, page 149); the Dutch counterresolution was rejected by the congress.

The position of workers in the event of war is defined in precise manner by the resolution of the Brussels Congress on militarism [see pages 35–36]. The international revolutionary Social Democracy in every country must rise with all its force against the chauvinist appetites of the ruling classes. It must consolidate ever more closely the bonds of solidarity between workers in every country. It must work unceasingly to conquer capitalism, which divides humanity into two great hostile camps and stirs up the people against each other.

With the disappearance of class domination, war will likewise disappear. The fall of capitalism means universal peace.

The representatives of the labor party in the deliberating meetings must reject all military credits; they must protest unceasingly against standing armies and demand disarmament. The whole of the socialist party must lend its support to all associations whose object is universal peace.

* * *

INTERNATIONAL ORGANIZATION
OF SOCIAL DEMOCRACY

Commission resolution presented to the congress. While this resolution was included in the official proceedings and is generally listed as one of the Zurich Congress resolutions, the plenary itself was not actually able to take it up due to lack of time.

Considering:

That it would be desirable for all Social Democrats to organize internationally under a common name, but that the restrictions upon liberty of association imposed by the reactionary laws of several countries prevent this for the time being:

This Congress recognizes as members of the international revolutionary Social Democratic party all organizations, societies, and parties that acknowledge the class war, and the necessity of the socialization of the means of production, and who are in accord with the principles of the International Socialist Workers' Congresses.

The Congress urges upon all members of the party and upon all labor organizations, trade or political, to agitate unceasingly for the abolition of all laws restricting the right of association.

The Congress expresses its wish that the first portion of the program of the Social Democratic Party of all countries, which sets forth its aims with regard to the necessary economic revolution, be stated in identical terms, as the aims of the Social Democracy of all countries are the same. The second part of the program will stand in accordance with the particular requirements and political demands of each country.

* * *

THE GENERAL STRIKE

Commission resolution, drafted by Karl Kautsky. While this resolution was included in the official proceedings and is generally listed as one of the Zurich Congress resolutions, the plenary itself was not actually able to take it up due to lack of time.

Whereas strikes cannot be successfully undertaken except in special cases and for a specific purpose, neither of which can be determined beforehand;

Whereas a general (international) strike is no longer practicable, owing to the very different economic development in different countries, and just so soon as it should become practicable it would become unnecessary;

Whereas even a general strike limited to one country cannot be successful; if it be conducted upon peaceful lines, the strikers will be the first to starve and would be compelled to capitulate; if on the other hand, it be conducted upon violent lines, the strikers would be ruthlessly butchered;

Therefore be it resolved:

That under existing social and political conditions, at best, a general strike of any one industry might be practicable.

Furthermore, general strikes might under certain circumstances be a very powerful weapon not only in the economic, but also in the political struggle. Nevertheless it is a weapon that, in order to be wielded with success, presupposes a powerful organization—both political and economic—of the working class.

Finally, the Congress recommends to the socialist political parties of all countries to promote with all possible energy such political and economic organization of the working class, and passes to the next order of business.

* * *

UNIVERSAL SUFFRAGE

Motion presented to the congress by the Austrian delegation and adopted by acclamation.

The Congress resolves that the time has come for the proletariat, in all countries in which the universal franchise has not yet been achieved, to launch an effort to achieve voting rights for all adults, regardless of gender or race. The proletariat of the entire world is urged to take part in this effort.

* * *

SOLIDARITY WITH BRITISH MINERS

Motion presented by the Austrian delegation and adopted by acclamation.

Hundreds of thousands of British miners are presently on strike for their basic rights.[2] Their struggle is in the interests of workers around the world. The Socialist Congress now meeting in Zurich expresses its support and its hope that the inception of this strike will lead to its complete victory.

* * *

MOTION ON FRENCH AND SIAMESE CRISIS

A number of Italian, German, and Swiss delegates asked the Congress to express its support to the French delegates, who are now engaged in an election campaign. The Congress adopted this proposal amid enthusiastic applause.

The British delegation reported on its unanimous decision to express solidarity with the French working class in the face of the enmity between France and Britain generated by their clash over Siam [Thailand].[3]

Regardless of enmity within the bourgeoisie, the interests of the working class in both France and Britain require a common struggle against capitalist exploitation. The British delegation therefore would like to express its warmest regards for the French workers, and to wish them every success in their election campaign.

4.

London Congress, July 27–August 1, 1896

The International Socialist Workers and Trade Union Congress of 1896 was the largest congress yet of the Second International, attended by around 770 delegates from twenty-two countries.

This was the last congress disrupted by anarchist delegates, who turned the event into "the most agitated, the most tumultuous, and the most chaotic of all the congresses of the Second Internacional," in the words of Émile Vandervelde.[1]

In the opening session, the congress voted to confirm the Zurich resolution on the conditions of admission, which excluded anarchists from attending. The vote was 17 national delegations to 2, with 1 delegation (Italy) abstaining. The French delegation (57 to 56) and Dutch (9 to 5) voted against; the British delegation supported the Zurich resolution by a vote of 223 to 104.

At the conclusion of the event, in a motion on the next congress, it was decided to definitively settle the question of anarchist participation at future international congresses, formally suspending them from membership in the International.

The London Congress was also the first one since the death of Frederick Engels the previous year. In his opening address to the congress, Paul Singer stated, "We, along with the whole of the Congress, express our deep regret that our great teacher, Frederick Engels, who, amidst the enthusiastic applause of the representatives of the workers of all countries, closed the last International Congress at Zurich, is no longer with us to open this, the greatest of all the Congresses that have been held. Frederick Engels is dead, but his spirit, his work, his example remain. The best thanks we can give him for his life of labour and self-sacrificing devotion is to follow in his footsteps, and carry on his work."[2]

THE AGRARIAN QUESTION

Report from the Agrarian Commission, as amended by the congress.

The evils that capitalistic exploitation, including landlordism, produce alike for the cultivator of the soil as for the whole of society at an ever-increasing rate, can be definitively abolished only in a society in which land, like the other means of production, has become socialized, i.e., common property, which society in its corporate capacity, causes to be cultivated in the common interest and on the most scientific methods.

The conditions of land tenure and the division of classes among the agricultural population in different countries are, however, too various for it to be possible to formulate a program that shall be binding for the labor parties of all countries as regards the means for attaining this end or the particular classes to be won over.

It is nonetheless the first duty of the labor parties throughout the world, insofar as the agrarian question is concerned, to organize all the subdivisions of the agricultural proletariat in its class struggle against its exploiters.

According to these principles, the Congress leaves it to every nation to formulate, for the attaining of this end, the ways and means most suitable to the situation of their country.

The Congress declares it desirable that, in every country where there are statistical committees appointed by the labor parties, they shall combine and centralize their results by communicating among themselves their statistical abstracts, etc.

* * *

POLITICAL ACTION

Report from the Political Action Commission, presented to the congress by George Lansbury. An amendment by members of the British delegation to delete the words "independent of and apart from all bourgeois political parties" from paragraph two was rejected.

This Congress understands political action as the organized struggle in all forms for the conquest of political power, and its use nationally and locally in legislation and administration by the working class on behalf of their emancipation.

The Congress declares that with the view of realizing the emancipation of the workers, the enfranchisement of humanity and the citizen, and the establishment of the international socialist republic, the conquest of political power is of paramount importance, and calls upon workers of all countries to unite, independent of and apart from all bourgeois political parties, and to demand universal adult suffrage, one adult one vote, and the second ballot, together with the national and local referendum and initiative.

The Congress also declares that the political emancipation of women is inseparable from that of the workers, and therefore calls upon women in all countries to work and organize politically side by side with the workers.

The Congress declares in favor of the full autonomy of all nationalities, and its sympathy with the workers of any country at present suffering under the yoke of military, national, or other despotisms; and calls upon the workers in all such countries to fall into line, side by side with the class-conscious workers of the world, to organize for the overthrow of international capitalism and the establishment of international social democracy.

This Congress declares that, whatever the pretext—whether it be religious or in the interests of so-called civilization—colonial extension is only another name for the extension of the area of capitalist exploitation in the exclusive interests of the capitalist class.

* * *

EDUCATION AND PHYSICAL DEVELOPMENT

Report from the Commission on Education and Physical Development, presented by Sidney Webb and amended by the congress.

In presenting their report to the Congress, the Commission on Education and Physical Development desire to express their sense of the enormous importance of the subject to the socialist movement and to the well-being of the working class of the whole world. Under the present system of capitalist exploitation, the children of the masses are stunted in their physical growth, deprived of that healthy leisure which is the condition of harmonious development, and prevented from obtaining access to the education and knowledge which is the common heritage of the whole human race. Under present circumstances the parents of the proletarian class [will] struggle in vain to secure to their children those opportunities of nurture and culture without which neither a healthy family nor a well-organized society is possible.

Further, the use by the capitalist employer of the labor of children and young persons to displace the labor of adults is a serious menace to the standard of living even of the best-organized workmen, whilst, by reducing the level of wages, it results in no pecuniary advantage even to the families concerned. Finally, seeing that the future well-being of society depends on the constant discovery of further scientific truths, especially in regard to economic, industrial, and social organization, socialists in all countries are urged to use their best efforts to promote scientific investigation and research of the highest kind, and to demand that the necessary means for such work be provided from public funds.

The following resolutions are submitted to the Congress:

RESOLUTIONS

1. That the Congress, whilst fully recognizing the value in education of independent experiment, declares that it is an essential duty of the public administration in each country to provide a complete system of education, under democratic public control, extending from the kindergarten to the university (including physical, scientific, artistic, and technical (manual work) training), the whole made generally accessible to every citizen by freedom from fees and public covering maintenance.

2. That the minimum age at which children should be exempted from full attendance at school, and legally allowed to be employed in industry, whether in factories or domestic workshops, should be gradually, but as quickly as possible, raised in all countries to at least sixteen years.[3]

3. That the employment of any child under eighteen in any trade proved to be unhealthy or dangerous, or in night work, be absolutely forbidden by law.

4. That in order to ensure proper continuance of educational training, and to restrain the illegitimate use of child labor by the capitalist, no employer be permitted to work any boy or girl under eighteen years of age, whether in factory or domestic workshops, for more than twenty-four hours per week (the half-time system), with compulsory attendance at continuation classes.

5. That, with regard to children, at any rate, the factory legislation of all industrial countries should be uniformly fixed by international agreement; and the Congress observes that the various governments have not

yet carried out the engagements to this effect solemnly entered into by them at the Berlin conference of 1891;[4] the British government, in particular, still permitting child labor at the age of eleven.

6. That for the proper protection and education of children in the industrial centers, it is absolutely necessary that manufacturing work done at home should be as effectively regulated and inspected as work done in factories; and where a capitalist employer, in order to escape from factory legislation, gives out work to be done in the workers' own homes, this Congress declares that he should be made legally responsible for seeing that such work is done under proper sanitary and other conditions, precisely as if it were done in his own factory.

* * *

INTERNATIONAL ORGANIZATION

Report from the Organization Commission, presented to the congress by Charles A. Gibson. The implementation of recommendations 1, 2, and 3 related to the future creation of the International Socialist Bureau.

In presenting their report to the Congress, the commission desires to state that of the resolutions sent in, they have been able to draw up in their report those which embody the desires of the framers of the majority of the resolutions. We have been unable to recommend the publication of an international paper as desired in resolutions 7 and 8, owing to the cost, and to the fact that many of our existing socialist papers contain reports from other countries.[5]

I

1. That in the opinion of this Congress an effort should immediately be made to create a permanent international committee, with a responsible secretary, centered in some convenient part of Europe.

2. That a small committee be appointed from this Congress to frame proposals for giving effect to no. 1, and report to the next Congress.

3. That said committee be empowered to act as a provisional committee for the movement between now and the next Congress; and that any nationality not represented on the committee by election from this Congress may send one representative to act until the international congress next meets.[6]

II

4. This Congress recognizes the constantly growing necessity of international economic information, and invites all nationalities to exercise their utmost diligence in carrying out the resolutions of Brussels and Zurich concerning the establishment of international bureaus of information [see pages 30–31 and 41–43].

III

5. In view of the large emigration from European countries to America and other continents, where a highly concentrated capitalism is thereby afforded extraordinary opportunities of reducing the wages of labor, and generally overcoming any resistance of the workers to oppression and degradation;

In view also of the fact that many of the emigrants, previously connected with the labor parties and labor organizations of their respective native lands, are generally failing (chiefly because of their ignorance of the English language) to connect themselves with the militant labor bodies of their adopted countries, so that the forces lost to the European movement by emigration are entirely lost to the international movement:

The Congress recommends that arrangements be made between the European countries and the Trans-Oceanic continents for the distribution among the emigrants at European ports and on board emigrant ships of printed leaflets containing necessary information and directions; also, for such socialist agitators as America and the other continents may require to properly organize the foreign portion of their proletariat.

* * *

WAR AND MILITARISM

Report from the War Commission, presented by Emmanuel Wurm and amended by the congress.

Under capitalism the chief causes of war are not religious or national differences but economic antagonisms, into which the exploiting classes of the various countries are driven by the system of production for profit.

Just as this system sacrifices unceasingly the life and health of the working class on the battlefield of labor, so it has no scruple in shedding their blood in search of profit by the opening up of new markets.

The working class of all countries should rise up against military oppression on the same ground that they revolt against all other forms of exploitation under which they are victimized by the possessing classes.

To attain this object they must acquire political power, so as to abolish the system of capitalist production, and simultaneously refuse, in all countries, to governments that are the instruments of the capitalist class, the means of maintaining the existing order of things.

Standing armies, whose maintenance even in times of peace exhausts the nation, and the cost of which is borne by the working class, increase the danger of war between nations, and at the same time favor the brutal oppression of the proletariat of the world. This is why the cry "Lay down your arms!" is no more listened to than the other appeals to humanitarian sentiments raised by the capitalist classes.

The working class alone has the serious desire, and it alone possesses the power, to realize universal peace.

It demands:

1. The simultaneous abolition of standing armies and the establishment of a national citizen force.

2. The establishment of an international tribunal of arbitration whose decision shall be final.

3. The final decision on the question of war or peace to be vested directly in the people in cases where the governments refuse to accept the decision of the tribunal of arbitration.

And it protests against the system of secret treaties.

The working class will only attain these objects by securing the control of legislation and by entering into an alliance with the international socialist movement, whereby peace may be finally assured, and the real fraternity of peoples permanently established.

* * *

THE ECONOMIC AND INDUSTRIAL QUESTION

Report from the Economic and Industrial Commission, presented to the congress by Hermann Molkenbuhr. A minority report from the commission, calling for discussion of the question of the general strike, was rejected; that resolution can be found in the appendix, pages 149–50.

I

In the opinion of this Congress, the workers of all nations should strive continuously as a class for the socialization of the means of production, transport, distribution, and exchange; the whole to be controlled by a completely democratic organization in the interests of the entire community, thus emancipating the laboring class and the people at large from the domination of capitalism. This Congress considers that national and international action in this complete socialist sense is becoming more necessary every day, in view of the disappearance of free competition and the rapid growth of national and international monopolies controlled by huge organizations of the capitalist class. Petroleum, oil, sewing cotton, certain minerals, large iron castings, etc., are now controlled by combinations of capitalists who aspire to fix both prices and wages in these trades. Such powerful corporations cannot be effectively countered by ordinary trade unions or isolated political action. A more complete organization of the workers is essential to overcome successfully the machinations of these great companies; and this Congress recommends that steps be taken to organize an international agency to call attention to the movements of these corporations, which frequently use political intrigues to further their ends, and should endeavor to bring about the socialization of such enterprises by national and international enactment.

In other directions the increasing power of mankind to produce wealth, instead of being turned to the advantage of the community, is proving [to be] the cause of gluts and commercial crises, national and international. The workers in coal, iron, leather, cotton, and other trades are in all countries thrown out of work and deprived of their livelihood by the action of economic causes which, so far, they have been unable to control. In all civilized nations the absolute need for the substitution of ownership by the community for such a chaotic system is being recognized; and the great coal mines, the great iron works and chemical works, the railways, and the larger factories have all reached the stage where their nationalization and socialization present no difficulty from the economic point of view.

This Congress, therefore, calls upon the workers of the world to proceed at once to urge definite measures of socialization, nationalization, and communization in their respective countries, keeping one another fully informed as to what each nationality is doing in this direction, so that whatever policy is resolved upon may be adopted, so far as possible, simultaneously.

II

The trade union struggle of the workers is indispensable to resist the economic tyranny of capital, and thereby better the actual condition of the toilers. Without trade unions no living wage and no shortening of hours of labor can be expected. By this struggle, however, the exploitation of labor will only be lessened, not abolished. The exploitation of labor can only be done away with entirely when society has taken control of all the means of production, including the land and the means of distribution. This, however, requires in the first instance a system of legislative measures. In order to carry out those measures completely, the working class should be the dominating political power, which depends on the standard of organization attained. The trade unions, therefore, help to consolidate the political power of the laboring classes by reason of their organizing efforts. The organization of the working class is incomplete and unfinished so long as it is political only.

But the economic struggle also calls for political action by the laboring class. Whatever the workers gain from their employers in open disputes must be confirmed by law in order to be maintained, while trade conflicts may in other cases be rendered superfluous by legislative measures.

The more the international organization and cooperation of the capitalist world market are perfected, the more the international cooperation of the working classes in regard to trade union action—more especially the protection of labor by law—becomes necessary.

In the near future international cooperation of the proletariat on the following lines will be necessary:

I. Abolition of all tariffs, duties on articles of consumption, and exportation premiums.

II. International factory and labor-protection laws.

Whereas in regard to the latter point, the resolutions of the Paris Congress are reaffirmed [see pages 22–24], the Congress resolves temporarily to limit the palliative legislation to:

(a) To demand the legal eight-hour day.

(b) To abolish the sweating system [sweatshops], and to introduce legislative protection for the workers who do not work in factories, workshops, etc.

(c) The recognition of the unassailable right of combination and co-alition of both sexes. Further, it is the duty of trade unions to admit as members women working in the particular trade and to try to carry out the principle of equal wages for equal work for both sexes, and also to admit apprentices in order to form them into a special section of adherents and in order to carry on their socialist and trade education.

The resolutions adopted at the Paris Congress were:

1. The legal eight-hour day, to which it is proposed to add that six hours' night work constitute an equivalent for eight hours' day work.

2. Abolition of child labor under the age of fourteen, and limitation of the working day to six hours a day for all between fourteen and fifteen.

3. Prohibition of night work, save in trades in which continuous running is a necessity.

4. Prohibition of night work for both sexes under the age of eighteen.

5. At least thirty-six hours of complete leisure in each week.

6. Prohibition of those industries and methods of production which specially injure the health of the workers.

7. Abolition of the truck system.[7]

8. The inspection of all industries—whether carried on in factories, small workshops, or at home—by paid inspectors, at least half of whom should be chosen by the workers.

To accomplish this, economic and political action must go hand in hand.

Therefore, the Congress declares the organization of the workers in trade unions to be an urgent matter in the struggle for the emancipation of the working class, and in connection with similar resolutions passed at the Brussels and Zurich congresses [see pages 31–32 and 41–43], considers it to be the duty of all workers who endeavor to liberate labor from the yoke of capitalism to join the unions in their respective trades.

In order to make the trade unions as effective as possible they are recommended to organize national trade unions in their respective countries, thus avoiding waste of power by small independent or local organizations. Especially, difference of political views ought not to be considered a reason for separate action in the economic struggle; on the other hand, the nature of the class struggle makes it the duty of the labor organizations to educate their fellow members up to the truths of Social Democracy.

Trade unions should also admit female workers into their ranks, and secure for them equal wages for the same kind and amount of work, and should not appeal for restrictive legislation against the immigration of aliens.

In the struggle for better wages and conditions of work, the trade unions ought to control the application of the existing laws for the protection of labor.

The Congress considers that strikes and boycotts are necessary weapons to attain the objects of trade unions. What is most essential is the thorough organization of the working classes, as the successful management of a strike depends on the strength of its organization.

In order to have a uniform international trade union movement, a central trade union commission should be constituted in every country. These commissions shall collect statistics about the labor market and shall exchange these statistics, together with other regular reports on important events in each country.

It should be the special duty of the trade unions of all countries to take care that workers coming from another country become members of the union of their respective trades and do not work for less than trade union wages.

In case of strikes, lockouts, and boycotts, the trade unions of all countries should assist one another according to their means.

III

The economic and industrial development is going on with such rapidity that a crisis may occur within a comparatively short time. The Congress, therefore, impresses upon the proletariat of all countries the imperative necessity for learning, as class-conscious citizens, how to administer the business of their respective countries for the common good.

Amendments to Economic and Industrial Reports adopted by Congress

(1) No woman to be allowed to work for six weeks before and after confinement, and to receive maintenance from a State Maternity Department during such term of prohibition (Mrs. Hicks). (2) The minimum age of child labor to be raised to sixteen years (Mr. Quelch). (3) Wherever private employment fails, public employment should be provided at the public cost (Dr. Pankhurst). (4) No restriction to be placed upon immigration (Jewish Workers). (5) The May Day demonstration to be a demonstration against militarism as well as in favor of the eight

hours (Swiss delegation). (6) Mutual efforts to be made against "alien" blacklegs in case of trade disputes (Mr. D. Hennessey). (7) Abolition of "home work" whenever possible (Mr. Herbert Burrows). (8) To include apprentices in unions, formed into a special group, and to give them a socialistic and technical education (French delegate).

* * *

MISCELLANEOUS RESOLUTIONS

Report from Commission on Miscellaneous Matters, presented to the congress by J. Bruce Glasier.

1. That this Congress declares the fundamental right of liberty of conscience, of speech, and of the press, and the right of public meeting and combination, both locally and internationally, of the workers and all other sections of the people for the attainment of political, industrial, and social change.

2. The Congress calls upon the workers to use their strongest efforts in their respective countries to obtain an amnesty for political prisoners; and expresses its condemnation of the system of police provocation of plots designed to bring discredit upon and provoke repressive measures against advanced movements; and further calls for the immediate exposure of and investigation into all cases concerning which suspicion exists that the convictions have been obtained by any such detestable methods.

3. That agencies by which the workers may obtain employment are a matter of public necessity, and should not be used for private speculation or profit-making, and in view of the gross abuse and corruption attached to employment registries conducted by private persons, the Congress urges the abolition of such registries, and demands the institution of free registries or labor bureaus conducted by the municipalities or bona fide trade unions.

4. Owing to the circumstance that the German, Austrian, Spanish, and several other sections have sent no delegation to this commission, it has been thought inadvisable to bring in any report on the subject of an international language; but it recommends that the chairman put the question from the chair to the Congress by nations as to which of the languages—English, French, or German—they would prefer to adopt;

none of the nations speaking these languages to vote when their own language is put to the meeting.[8]

***

THE NEXT CONGRESS

Motion by Wilhelm Liebknecht for the Bureau (Standing Orders Committee), as amended by the congress. The most significant aspect of this resolution was a decision by the Second International to exclude anarchists from all future international congresses.

The Standing Orders Committee of the Congress is entrusted with the duty of drawing up the invitation for the next congress by appealing exclusively to:

1. The representatives of those organizations that seek to substitute socialist property and production for capitalist property and production, and which consider legislative and parliamentary action as one of the necessary means of attaining that end.

2. Purely trade [union] organizations which, though taking no militant part in politics, declare that they recognize the necessity of legislative and parliamentary action; consequently anarchists are excluded.

Each nationality shall verify the credentials of its delegates, with right of appeal, to a special commission elected by all the nationalities represented at the congress. The credentials of all nationalities sending less than five delegates to be referred to the Credentials Commission to deal with in the same way as disputed credentials.

Resolved that the next congress be held in Germany in the year 1899. In case it should be impossible to hold the congress in Germany, it is decided that it shall be held in Paris in the year 1900.

***

SOLIDARITY WITH SOCIALIST MAYOR OF LILLE

Motion by James Leakey, adopted by acclamation.

That the delegates assembled at this Congress express their sympathy with Citizen Delory, suspended from his functions as mayor of Lille by the reactionary prefect of the department, on account of disturbances intentionally fomented by the Clerical Party, and [the delegates] encourage the socialist municipality of Lille to continue the good work they have begun.[9]

***

PROTEST AGAINST ANTILABOR RULING

Motion by W. Stevenson, adopted by acclamation.

That this Congress of representative workers records the expression of its indignation at the abominable observations of Justice Grantham yesterday, in the action against the trade union officials of the pianoforte trade, wherein he describes workmen joining a trade society as obtaining the strength of brute beasts depriving them of reasoning power.[10]

***

THE FIGHT AGAINST RUSSIAN TSARISM

Motion by Swiss delegation, adopted by acclamation.

The Congress notes the eminently remarkable fact that has never yet occurred, viz., the representation of Russian working-class organizations at an international congress.[11] It hails with joy this fresh awakening of the proletarian movement, and in the name of the working-class fighting the good fight wishes for its Russian brethren courage and indefatigable perseverance in their fight against bitter tyranny. The organization of the Russian working class is the best guarantee against tsarism, one of the last strongholds of European reaction.

***

GREETINGS TO BULGARIAN SOCIAL DEMOCRATS

Motion by Bulgarian delegation, adopted unanimously.

That the Congress send its fraternal greetings to the Third National Congress of the Bulgarian Social Democratic Workers Party, which meets on Sunday, August 2 at Sofia.

* * *

VIOLENCE AGAINST IMMIGRANT WORKERS

Motion by Italian delegation, adopted unanimously.

Seeing that the recent regrettable riots at Zurich are the result of the economic and moral servitude under which the greater part of the Italian immigrant workers live under capitalism,[12] the Congress declares that the results of that economic competition of the workers, which prevents the solidarity of the proletariat, can only be got rid of by the propagation and organization of socialism.

* * *

REMEMBRANCE OF FIRST INTERNATIONAL

Motion by Alfred Léon Gérault-Richard, adopted by the congress.

That the Congress record its respectful and grateful remembrance of those who more than thirty years ago founded, in this very town of London, the International.[13]

* * *

SOLIDARITY WITH CUBA, CRETE, AND MACEDONIA

Motion by Paul Argyriadès, adopted by acclamation.

The French delegation, having carried a resolution in favor of those struggling for emancipation in Cuba, Crete, and Macedonia, asks the Congress to vote its wishes for the emancipation of these three nations who are struggling for their political and economic liberty.[14]

5.

Paris Congress, September 23–27, 1900

The Second International's 1900 congress in Paris was attended by almost 1,400 delegates (over 1,000 from France alone) from twenty-one countries.

Since the previous congress four years earlier, the political divisions within the world socialist and labor movement had sharpened considerably, highlighted by two controversies.

The first involved Eduard Bernstein, a follower and collaborator of Marx and Engels when they were alive. In the late 1890s, however, Bernstein became increasingly critical of Marxism's political conclusions; these criticisms were codified in his 1899 book, *Evolutionary Socialism*. In this work, Bernstein openly rejected the revolutionary aims of the socialist movement. In his words, "The ultimate aim of socialism is nothing, but the movement is everything."[1] Furthermore, Bernstein expressed the opinion that revolution was no longer a strategic necessity, as he believed that capitalism had acquired the potential to ameliorate or eliminate the contradictions and crises that Marx and Engels had pointed to. The perspective Bernstein outlined came to be known within the socialist movement as "revisionism."

Bernstein's challenge found an echo in some sectors of the socialist movement, giving rise to sharp polemics and debates, as many prominent socialists forcefully defended Marxism's revolutionary foundations. In October 1899 a congress of the German Social Democratic Party (SPD) formally condemned Bernstein's views by a vote of 216 to 21. The lopsidedness of that vote, however, did not reflect the real support for Bernstein's views within the SPD. Many members and officials supported some of the conclusions reached by Bernstein, but were reluctant to express those opinions openly.

The second controversy concerned Alexandre Millerand, a member of the Independent Socialist group in the French parliament. In June 1899 Millerand accepted a position in the capitalist government of France as minister of commerce. This move led to a wide-ranging debate in the working-class movement, given that socialists had always rejected accepting posts in capitalist governments.

The Millerand affair gave rise to the main debate at the 1900 Paris Congress.

Karl Kautsky presented a resolution that condemned socialist participation in capitalist governments under "normal" circumstances, but left the door open to it under "exceptional" ones. "If in some special instance the political situation necessitates this dangerous expedient," Kautsky's resolution stated, "that is a question of tactics and not of principle." The intention of Kautsky in making this motion, as he subsequently declared, was to defend a revolutionary perspective while seeking socialist unity.[2]

Counterposed to the Kautsky resolution was one put forward by Enrico Ferri and Jules Guesde, opposing such participation under all circumstances. (That resolution can be found in the appendix, on page 150.) A long debate on this question took place in a commission and on the floor of the congress itself. At the debate's conclusion, the Kautsky resolution received 29 votes, against 9 for the Guesde-Ferri resolution.

Nevertheless, the ambiguities of the Kautsky resolution, and the dissatisfaction it engendered, meant that the question would inevitably come up again. It did so at the next international congress in 1904, where the conclusions of the Guesde-Ferri resolution were largely accepted, eliminating the "exceptional circumstances" clause.

The key organizational decision of the Paris Congress was the creation of the International Socialist Bureau (ISB) as the executive leadership body of the Second International, as had been urged at the 1896 congress (see page 54–55). Prior to 1900, the Second International functioned solely as a loose association that met in congresses every two to four years, with no powers to implement decisions or even share information. After 1900 the ISB, based in Brussels, functioned as a center for correspondence and information, responsible for maintaining liaison between parties, making technical preparations, and setting agendas for congresses.

Also established by the congress was an Interparliamentary Committee, consisting of socialist deputies in parliament, in order "to facilitate common action on the big international political and economic questions."

INTERNATIONAL ORGANIZATION

Resolution of the First Commission, presented to the congress by Hendrick Van Kol. The resolution outlined the structure and tasks of the International Socialist Bureau that was being formed.

I

The International Socialist Congress of Paris:

Considering that international congresses, which will become the parliament of the proletariat, should pass resolutions that guide the proletariat in its struggle;

Considering that these resolutions, a result of international agreement, should be translated into acts;

Decides to take the following steps:

1. An organizing committee shall be selected as soon as possible by the socialist organizations of the country where the next congress is to be held.

2. A permanent international committee, having two delegates for each country, shall be formed, and shall have charge of the necessary funds. It shall settle the agenda, and shall call for reports from each nationality adhering to the congress.

3. This committee shall appoint a paid general secretary, who shall:

(a) Obtain the necessary information.

(b) Draw up a code explaining the resolutions taken at previous congresses.

(c) Distribute the reports on the socialist movement of each country two months before each new congress.

(d) Draw up a summary of the reports discussed at the congress.

(e) Publish from time to time pamphlets and manifestos on pressing questions, as well as on important reforms and studies on important political and economic questions.

(f) Take necessary means to improve the action and the international organization of the proletariat in every country.

The permanent international committee and the secretary-general will be based in Brussels.

II

The International Socialist Committee will require socialist members of parliament in each country to form a special interparliamentary commission to facilitate common action on the big international political and economic questions. This commission will be assisted by the International Socialist Committee.

III

The international secretariat based in Brussels will be charged with creating an archive of international socialism, composed of books, documents, and reports concerning the workers' movement in different countries.

* * *

WORKDAY LIMITS AND MINIMUM WAGE

Resolution of the Second Commission, presented to the congress by Emmanuel Wurm from Germany and Charles Gheude from Belgium.

I

The Congress, in accordance with the decision of previous international congresses, considers that the limitation of the working day must continue to be the object of ceaseless efforts by all workers, and declares that the daily duration of labor must be fixed by law at the provisional maximum of eight hours for workers of all countries and all industries.

It therefore urges working-class organizations to pursue this object by persistent and escalating agitation and by united trade union and political action.

II

The Congress declares that a minimum wage is possible only where it can be set by well-organized trade unions; that this minimum cannot be the same for all countries, but depends on local conditions.

It urges workers to seek the achievement of this reform by using the most practical and appropriate means, based on the economic and industrial condition of each region, as well as its political and administrative situation.

It recommends, as a first step in obtaining this demand, that governments and public bodies should be pressed to establish a minimum wage to be paid directly by the public authority, or else by entrepreneurs doing business with it.

* * *

EMANCIPATION OF LABOR AND
EXPROPRIATION OF THE BOURGEOISIE

Resolution of the Third Commission, presented to the congress by Wilhelm Ellenbogen and adopted unanimously.

I

The modern proletariat is the necessary result of the capitalist system of production, which requires the political and economic exploitation of labor by capital.

Its elevation and emancipation can be realized only by entering into antagonism with the defenders of the interests of capitalism, which by its very constitution must lead inevitably to the socialization of the means of production.

Facing the capitalist class, the proletariat must therefore present itself as a fighting class.

Socialism, which has been given the task of constituting the proletariat into an army for this class war, has for its duty, above all, to awaken in it by careful, incessant, and methodical propaganda the consciousness of its own interests and strength, and to use for this objective all the means that the existing political and social situation may place in its hands, and that its higher conception of justice may suggest.

Among these means the Congress suggests political action, universal suffrage, the organization of the proletariat into political groups, trade unions, cooperative societies, mutual assistance societies, circles of art and education, etc. It urges the active socialist movement to do everything possible to combine these means of struggle and education that augment the power of the working class, and will render it capable of expropriating the bourgeoisie, both politically and economically, and of socializing the means of production.

II

The socialists of all countries undertake to use every means in their power to secure for the foreign workers in their respective countries the same right of combination as is possessed by the inhabitants themselves.

* * *

THE FIGHT AGAINST MILITARISM AND WAR

Resolution of the Fourth Commission, presented to the congress by Rosa Luxemburg. It was adopted unanimously.

I

The Congress declares that in all countries militarism should be opposed daily with zeal, energy, and vigor, and that proletarians of all countries should unite against the alliance of the bourgeoisie and of imperialist governments.

The Congress advises that:

1. The different socialist parties should carefully instruct and organize the youth in the fight against militarism.

2. Socialist deputies in all countries should vote against military and naval expenditures, especially in cases of colonial aggression.

3. The permanent International Socialist Committee should organize in all countries a common and combined antimilitarist agitation and movement of protest.

The Congress protests against so-called peace conferences, similar to that of The Hague, which in present-day society can only lead to disasters, as has been seen recently in the war in the Transvaal.

II

1. The Paris Congress condemns the savage policy of oppression of Russian tsarism towards the Polish and Finnish peoples,[3] and urges the proletarians of all nationalities suffering under the yoke of absolute rule to unite for the common struggle against the common enemy of democracy and socialism.

2. The Congress condemns the atrocities of the British government against the Boers of South Africa.[4]

3. The Congress again affirms its belief in the sympathetic and fraternal feelings that should unite all nations, and denounces the misrule, cruelty, and massacres in Armenia. It also condemns the criminal complicity of the various capitalist governments, and urges socialist parliamentary deputies to intervene on behalf of the cruelly oppressed Armenian people, to whom the Congress gives its ardent solidarity.[5]

* * *

COLONIAL POLICY

Resolution of the Fifth Commission, presented to the congress by Hendrick Van Kol.

The International Socialist Congress held in Paris in 1900:

Considering that the development of capitalism leads inevitably to colonial expansion, a cause of conflicts between governments;

Considering that imperialism, which results therefrom, excites chauvinism in all countries, and forces ever-increasing expenditures to the profit of militarism;

Considering that the colonial policy of the bourgeoisie has no other object than to increase the profits of the capitalist class and to maintain the existence of the capitalist system, while sapping the lifeblood and exhausting the resources of the proletariat, and by committing innumerable crimes and cruelties towards the indigenous races of the colonies conquered by armed force;

The Congress declares:

That the organized proletariat ought to use all the means in its power to combat colonial expansion of the bourgeoisie, and to expose categorically and vehemently the injustices and cruelties that inevitably spring from it in all parts of the world, given up to the greed of a shameless and remorseless capitalism.

With this end in view, the Congress specifies more specifically the following steps:

1. That the various socialist parties apply themselves to the study of the colonial question wherever the economic conditions admit it.

2. To especially encourage the formation of colonial socialist parties affiliated to organizations in the metropolitan countries.

3. To create friendly relations between the socialist parties of different colonies.

* * *

ORGANIZATION OF MARITIME WORKERS

Resolution of the Sixth Commission, presented by Albert Störmer from Germany and adopted unanimously.

The members of the commission considered the organization of maritime workers in the broadest sense, as involving not just sailors at sea, but also workers on the docks.

Based on the nature of their employment, these two sectors of workers are most directly in contact with other countries, with wages paid by other sectors or branches of industry. For this reason, the commission was aware that the organization of these workers, and resolving their most immediate grievances through legislation, should receive the attention of socialist parties united internationally.

The poor conditions facing these two sectors of workers on the job do not need to be listed here; they are known by all. At the same time, it is necessary to show that the bourgeois parties of all countries have done nothing to remedy the ills.

Given that special laws concerning the merchant marine exist in all countries, the commission felt that it is the special duty of organized socialist parties, as long as capitalism lasts, to see to it that all the laws on work in this industry are fully complied with.

At the same time, the commission was aware that sailors need to organize in unions and political groups, recognize the class struggle, and utilize their votes to obtain socialist representatives who will not stop fighting for their interests.

Recognizing the special difficulties of fully organizing sailors, the congress should insist that all trade unions and socialist parties help sailors to organize. Within their countries, there should not be separate organizations for sailors, but rather dockworkers' unions should seek to recruit them.

The immediate demands of sailors, for which parliaments should be pressed to act, are the following:

1. All private offices for the hiring of sailors should be abolished, and these offices should be free at all ports—i.e., no fees should be levied—and they should be under the control of workers' organizations.

2. Hotels for sailors should be established under the combined control of trade unions and municipal authorities, but the sailors should not be influenced in any way.

3. Special courts should be established, some of the judges being workers, so that disputes arising during the voyage may be settled. The power of punishment given to officers at sea should be curtailed.

4. A maximum number of hours constituting a working day should be set, and all extra work paid for as overtime. Only indispensable work shall be done on Sundays and holidays.

5. Compensation shall be paid for injuries received by sailors when at sea; in cases of death, dependents of the deceased shall be provided for.

6. There shall be a minimum wage for sailors.

7. Laws are necessary assuring complete and impartial inspection, with a view toward preventing accidents. Suitable provisions will be adopted for all those at sea. Ships shall be fully staffed, with consideration given to knowledge of languages, so that sailors can understand commands.

8. Laws are needed concerning food and sleeping accommodations, and especially sanitary and hygienic precautions.

9. No sailor shall be allowed to be hired outside of the laws and regulations affecting him.

10. A sufficient number of inspectors shall be named, assigned to visit each and every ship at port, having the powers necessary to detain all ships lacking satisfactory conditions and in which laws would be violated in any fashion.

As to dockworkers, we recommend:

1. Compensation shall be paid in all cases of accidents. No insurance premium will be paid out by workers for this; that is the responsibility of employers, whether on the docks or at sea.

2. All gear and machinery shall be periodically inspected so as to prevent accidents.

3. Wages shall never be paid in public houses or registry offices.

4. A labor bureau shall be established at every port for the hiring of workers.

5. There shall be a maximum number of hours and a minimum wage. Higher wages shall be paid for night and Sunday work.

In order to accomplish these goals, the Congress recommends that all sailors and dockworkers join the International Federation of Dock Workers, through which they will be in continuous contact, and will be in a position to take group action to fight for their demands.[6]

* * *

UNIVERSAL SUFFRAGE AND POPULAR SOVEREIGNTY

Resolution of the Seventh Commission, presented to the congress by Engelbert Pernerstorfer.

1. Universal, direct, and secret suffrage is for workers' democracy one of the essential means of obtaining political and social emancipation.

2. In cases where peoples are deprived of parliamentary representation, or where this representation does not yet rest on any principles, the Congress urges them to struggle for the conquest and full application of universal suffrage.

The Congress considers the fight for the introduction of universal suffrage, as well as the exercise of this right, to be one of the most effective means of education of the proletariat in public life.

3. The Congress considers that men and women have equal rights, and is in favor of universal suffrage for both sexes.

4. Where universal suffrage exists, the Congress declares that the duty of socialists is to advocate for the application of proportional representation.

5. The Congress is in favor of popular initiatives and referenda, as it considers that the people are sovereign and that direct legislation by the people is an attribute of that sovereignty

6. The Congress considers that the struggle for the improvement of universal suffrage is one of the best means of educating the masses intellectually and morally, so that they may obtain permanent political and economic sovereignty and may thus be prepared for governing the socialist state of the future.

* * *

MUNICIPAL SOCIALISM

Resolution of the Eighth Commission, presented to the congress by Émile Vinck.

Whereas the term "municipal socialism" does not signify a special kind of socialism, but simply the application of the general principles of socialism to a particular department of political activity;[7]

Whereas reforms connected therewith are not and cannot be put forward as the realization of the collectivist society, but are put forward as playing a part in a sphere of action that socialists can and should seize upon in order to prepare and facilitate the coming of the collectivist society;

Whereas the municipality can become an excellent laboratory of decentralized economic activity, and at the same time a formidable political fortress for the use of local socialist majorities against the bourgeois majority of the central power, once substantial autonomous powers have been obtained;

The Congress declares:

That it is the duty of all socialists, without misunderstanding the importance of the wider political issues, to make clear to all the value of municipal activity, to recognize in all municipal reforms the importance that attaches to them as "embryos of the collectivist society," and to endeavor to municipalize such public services as the urban transport service, education, shops, bakeries, medical assistance, hospitals, water supply, baths and washhouses, the food supply and clothing, dwellings for the people, power supply, public works, the police force, etc., etc., to see that these public services shall be model services as much from the point of view of the interests of the community as from that of the citizens who serve it;

That the local bodies which are not large enough to undertake themselves any of these reforms should federate with one another for such purposes;

That in countries where the political system does not allow municipalities to adopt this course, it is the duty of socialists serving on such bodies to endeavor to obtain for municipal authorities sufficient liberty and independence to obtain these reforms.

The Congress further decides that the time has come to convene an international congress of socialist municipal councilors.

Such a congress should have a double purpose:

(a) To make publicly known what reforms have been secured in the area of municipal administration, and what moral and financial advantages have resulted.

(b) To establish a national bureau in each country and an international bureau, entrusted with the task of collecting all the information and documents relating to municipal life, so as to facilitate the study of municipal questions.[8]

The Congress also decides that the business of convening this so-cialist municipal congress shall be left in the hands of the permanent international bureau.

***

SOCIALISTS IN PUBLIC OFFICE AND ALLIANCES WITH BOURGEOIS PARTIES (KAUTSKY RESOLUTION)

Resolution of the Ninth Commission, drafted by Karl Kautsky and known generally as the "Kautsky resolution." Reports to the congress were made by Émile Vandervelde for the commission majority and Enrico Ferri for the commission minority, which had presented a motion by Ferri and Jules Guesde. (For the text of the Guesde-Ferri resolution, see the appendix, page 150.) The Kautsky resolution was adopted by a vote of 24 to 4 in the commission, and 29 to 9 by the full congress. The main conclusions of the Guesde-Ferri resolution regarding socialist participation in capitalist governments, however, were largely accepted by the 1904 Amsterdam Congress, eliminating the Kautsky resolution's "exceptional circumstances" clause.

I

In a modern democratic state the conquest of political power by the proletariat cannot be effected by a *coup de main*, but must be the result of a long and toilsome work of proletarian organization, political and economic, of the physical and moral regeneration of the working class, and of the gradual conquest of municipal and legislative assemblies.

But in a country where governmental power is centralized, it cannot be conquered in a fragmentary manner.

The entry of an isolated socialist into a bourgeois government cannot be regarded as the normal commencement of the conquest of political power, but only as a compulsory expedient, transitory and exceptional.

If in some special instance the political situation necessitates this dangerous expedient, that is a question of tactics and not of principle; the International Congress is not called upon to pronounce on that point. But in any case, the entry of a socialist into a bourgeois government affords no hope of good results for the militant proletariat unless the great majority of the Socialist Party approves of this step and the socialist minister remains the delegate of his party.

In the contrary case, in which such a minister becomes independent of the party or represents only a section of it, his intervention in a bourgeois ministry threatens disorganization and confusion to the militant proletariat, threatens to weaken rather than to strengthen it, and hinders rather than advances the proletarian conquest of public powers.

In any case, the Congress is of the opinion that, even in the most exceptional circumstances, a socialist ought to quit the ministry whenever the latter gives any proof of partiality in the struggle between capital and labor. No minister delegated by the Socialist Party can continue to participate in the government if the party concludes that this government has not observed absolute impartiality in the relations between capital and labor.

II

The Congress reasserts that the class struggle forbids all alliances with any fraction whatever of the capitalist class.

Even admitting that exceptional circumstances may sometimes render coalitions necessary (without confusion of party or tactics), these coalitions, which the party should seek to reduce to the smallest possible number until they entirely disappear, must not be permitted except insofar as their necessity is recognized by the district or national organization to which the groups concerned belong.

* * *

THE FIRST OF MAY

Resolution of the Tenth Commission, presented to the congress by Theodor Bömelburg.

The Congress adheres to the decisions taken by previous congresses as to the demonstrations on the First of May; it considers that these actions are evidence of a desire for an eight-hour day, and that taking off work on this day is the most effective form of demonstration.

* * *

TRUSTS

Resolution of the Eleventh Commission, presented to the congress by F. M. Wibaut and adopted unanimously.

Partial trusts are coalitions of owners of industry and commerce, formed to increase their profits.

These coalitions are the inevitable consequence of competition in a system of production and of distribution whose aim is not production as such, but exclusively to obtain profits for the owners. The growth of the means of production creates ways of obtaining a greater mass of products than is possible to be sold. Since competition tends to diminish profits, it is inevitable that under the present system every effort should be made to eliminate competition and for the owners to come to an agreement among themselves. In this way trusts are inevitable. Trusts, therefore, are, in a sense, a higher form of production, by making production—for profit—more rational and economical, avoiding the waste of overproduction, reducing transport costs, cutting expenses for advertising and sale, and payments to intermediaries.

On the other hand, trusts have a tendency to cause prices to rise, by avoiding the fall in prices that comes from improved production. Moreover, their goal is to increase the oppression of workers, opposing unions and attempts by the labor force to organize against the united power of the owners.

Pools and coalitions are simply tools of the trusts and cartels, operating solely to raise prices on the necessities of life. These increases constitute a disaster for the general interest of the population, and must be vigorously condemned.

While the Congress wishes to show what trusts do to workers, it does not however recommend their prohibition, as they are a logical result of the present system of production. Legislation, at best, could modify their form, but it cannot hinder their activity. Socialists, nevertheless, do not oppose laws compelling trusts to reveal their operations and their financial results.

The only remedy is nationalization, and afterwards an international regularization of production.

Proletarian action should be directed toward ameliorating political and economic conditions. Use should be made of cooperation [cooperatives], by which the public expropriation of the great branches of production that trusts have made possible may be brought about. Thus, private production, having profit as its aim, will be gradually transformed into social production, which will look upon production for use as its aim.

* * *

THE GENERAL STRIKE

Resolution of the Twelfth Commission. Reporters were Karl Legien for the commission majority and Aristide Briand for the commission minority, with disagreements along the lines of debates on this question at previous congresses. The congress adopted the majority resolution, which follows, by a vote of 27 to 7.

The Congress, taking into account the resolutions adopted by the international congresses of Paris and Zurich, and recalling the resolution adopted in London in 1896 that dealt with the general strike:[9]

Considers that strikes and boycotts are necessary weapons to attain the goals of the working class, but it does not see how an international general strike is, under existing circumstances, possible.

What is immediately necessary is the organization of trade unions by the masses of workers, since it is only the extension of organization that makes possible strikes in entire industries or entire countries.

6.

Amsterdam Congress, August 14–20, 1904

By 1904 world capitalism had undergone a significant transformation. A handful of imperialist powers were in the process of carving up the world, with sharpening conflicts among themselves over how to divide the booty. The phenomenon of imperialist war was becoming a central part of the world picture. Among these conflicts were the Spanish-American War of 1898 and the subsequent insurgency in the Philippines, the Boer War beginning in 1899, and the Russo-Japanese War, which began in early 1904.

This world development left its mark on the Amsterdam Congress, attended by almost 450 delegates from twenty-five countries.

The main debate at the congress concerned the same question that had dominated the 1900 congress: the issue of socialist participation in bourgeois governments. There were two main counterposed resolutions.

The first of these was based on a resolution adopted by the Social Democratic Party of Germany at its 1903 congress in Dresden, which unambiguously condemned all socialist participation in capitalist governments. At the Amsterdam Congress, this same resolution was put forward, presented as the "Dresden-Amsterdam resolution."

Counterposed to this was a resolution presented by Victor Adler and Émile Vandervelde. Endorsing the ambiguities of the Kautsky resolution adopted by the Paris Congress four years earlier (see pages 77–78), the Adler-Vandervelde resolution stated, "That the Social Democracy, in regard of the dangers and the inconveniences of the participation in the government in bourgeois society, brings to mind and confirms the Kautsky resolution, passed at the International Congress of Paris in 1900."

The debate over these counterposed resolutions dominated the congress proceedings, highlighted by a verbal duel between August Bebel, on behalf of the Dresden-Amsterdam resolution, and Jean Jaurès, on behalf of the Adler-Vandervelde resolution.

In the congress commission taking up the question, the Adler-Vandervelde resolution was rejected by a vote of 24 to 16. The Dresden-Amsterdam resolution was then adopted by 27 votes to 3, with 10 abstentions. But when the question reached the congress floor, the vote was considerably closer. The Adler-Vandervelde resolution failed—but only by a tie vote of 21 to 21. (For the text of the Adler-Vandervelde resolution, see the appendix, page 151.) The Dresden-Amsterdam resolution was then adopted by a vote of 25 to 5, with 12 abstentions.

While the Dresden-Amsterdam resolution did not specifically criticize the 1900 resolution, it annulled a major piece of the earlier document by eliminating that resolution's "exceptional circumstances" clause. But the closeness of the congress vote indicated the growing strength of the opportunist wing within the Second International.

The growth of reformist and opportunist tendencies was reflected elsewhere at the congress.

In the Commission on Immigration and Emigration, a debate occurred between a majority of the commission, which held the traditional socialist position of opposing all immigration restrictions, and a minority that adapted to anti-immigrant sentiment. (For the text of both resolutions, see the appendix, pages 151–53.) Both resolutions from the commission were withdrawn after they reached the congress floor, to be discussed at the next congress.

A similar division was seen on the question of colonialism. Prior to the Amsterdam Congress, the Dutch party had submitted a resolution on colonialism, presumably drafted by Hendrick Van Kol, presenting the perspective of a "socialist colonialism." This resolution (see the appendix, pages 153–55) was not discussed at the congress, and Van Kol himself presented the commission's resolution to the plenary, a resolution that strongly condemned capitalist colonial practices. But at the end of his report, Van Kol slipped in the remark that "a socialist state would also have colonies."[1] That same perspective is also embodied in the motion approved by the congress without discussion concerning British India (see pages 89–90).

The colonialism issue, too, would resurface at the 1907 congress in Stuttgart, where it would be the subject of a heated debate.

ON TACTICS (DRESDEN-AMSTERDAM RESOLUTION)

The resolution below was originally drafted by August Bebel, Karl Kautsky, and Paul Singer for the congress of the Social Democratic Party of Germany held in Dresden in September 1903. It was adopted there incorporating an amendment by Emmanuel Wurm and forty others that unambiguously condemned socialist participation in capitalist governments. The Dresden resolution was then submitted to the Second International's Amsterdam Congress by the Socialist Party of France, where it became known as the Dresden-Amsterdam resolution. The congress commission in Amsterdam taking up the question also had before it a counterresolution by Victor Adler and Émile Vandervelde. (For the text, see the appendix, page 151.) The commission rejected the Adler-Vandervelde resolution by a vote of 24 to 16, and then approved the Dresden-Amsterdam resolution by a vote of 27 to 3, with 10 abstentions. Following a debate by the full congress, the Adler-Vandervelde resolution also failed, but this time only by the narrowest of margins: a tie vote of 21 to 21. The Dresden-Amsterdam resolution was then adopted by a vote of 25 to 5, with 12 abstentions.

The Congress condemns most energetically the revisionist attempts, in the direction of changing our tried and victorious tactics based on the class struggle, and of replacing the conquest of the public powers through the supreme struggle with the bourgeoisie by a policy of concession to the established order.

The consequence of such revisionist tactics would be to change us from a party seeking the swiftest possible transformation of bourgeois society into socialist society—from a party strictly revolutionary in the best sense of the word—into a party contenting itself with the reform of bourgeois society.

Therefore the Congress, convinced, contrary to the present revisionist tendencies, that class antagonisms, far from diminishing, are intensifying, declares:

1. That the party disclaims any responsibility whatever for the political and economic conditions based on capitalist production, and consequently could not approve any methods tending to maintain the ruling class in power.

2. That the Social Democracy could accept no share in the government within capitalist society, as was definitely declared by the Kautsky resolution adopted by the international congress of Paris in 1900.

The Congress moreover condemns any attempt made to veil the ever-growing class antagonism, for the purpose of facilitating an understanding with bourgeois parties.

The Congress looks to the socialist parliamentary group to avail itself of its increased power—increased both by the greater number of its members and by the substantial growth of the body of electors behind it—to persevere in its propaganda toward the final goal of socialism, and, in conformity with our program, to defend most resolutely the interests of the working class, the extension and consolidation of its political liberties, to demand equality of rights for all; to continue with more energy than ever the struggle against militarism, against the colonial and imperialistic policy, against all manner of injustice, slavery, and exploitation; and, finally, to set itself energetically to improve social legislation to make it possible for the working class to accomplish its political and civilizing mission.

* * *

PARTY UNITY

Resolution presented by August Bebel, Karl Kautsky, Victor Adler, Edward Anseele, Enrico Ferri, Pieter Troelstra, and Émile Vandervelde, and adopted unanimously by the congress. In the commission discussion, Rosa Luxemburg submitted an amendment, which does not appear to have been voted on, stating that socialist unity can be achieved only on the basis of the class struggle.[2]

The Congress declares:

That in order for the working class to develop its full strength in the struggle against capitalism, it is necessary that there should be but one Socialist Party in each country as against the parties of capitalists, just as there is but one proletariat in each country.

For these reasons, it is the imperative duty of all comrades and all socialist organizations to strive to the utmost of their power to bring about this unity of the party, on the basis of the principles established by international congresses, this unity that is necessary in the interests of the proletariat. They are responsible for the disastrous consequences of the continuation of divisions within their ranks.

To assist in the attainment of this aim, the International Socialist Bureau, as well as all parties within the countries where this unity exists, will cheerfully offer their services and cooperation.

* * *

THE GENERAL STRIKE

This resolution, submitted by the Dutch delegation, was presented to the congress by Henriette Roland-Holst and adopted by a vote of 36 to 4, with 3 abstentions. As with resolutions adopted at previous international congresses, the resolution largely dismisses even the possibility of a general strike. Alternate resolutions with different appreciations of the general strike's prospects and importance were submitted by French delegates and by Raphael Friedeberg from Berlin.

The Congress, considering that it is desirable to define the position of the Social Democracy in regard to the "general strike";

Declares:

(a) that the prime necessity for a successful strike on a large scale is a strong organization and a self-imposed discipline of the working class;

(b) That the absolute "general strike," in the sense that *all* workers shall at a given moment lay down their work, would defeat its own object, because it would render all existence, including that of the proletariat, impossible; and

(c) That the emancipation of the working class cannot be the result of any such sudden exertion of force. Although, on the other hand, it is quite possible that a strike that spreads over a few economically important concerns, or over a large number of branches of trade, may be a means of bringing about important social changes, or of opposing reactionary designs on the rights of the workers; and

Therefore warns the workers not to allow themselves to be taken in tow by the anarchists, with their propaganda of the general strike, carried on with the object of diverting the workers from the really essential struggle that must be continued day by day by means of the trade unions, political action, and cooperatives; and

Calls upon the workers to build up their unity and power in the class struggle by perfecting their organization, because if the strike should appear at any time useful or necessary for the attainment of some political object, its success will entirely depend on that.

***

THE FIRST OF MAY

Commission resolution presented to the congress plenary by C. M. Olsen.

Whereas the demonstration of the workers on the First of May has for its object the common upholding—on a fixed day and in all the countries where there is a modern working-class movement—of the cause of the proletariat, especially the protection of workers by an eight-hour-day law, of class demands and universal peace, and of demonstrating the unity of the working-class movement and its demands in all countries;

Whereas the unity of the demonstration exists only in some countries; and in other countries not the First of May, but the first Sunday in the month, is celebrated:

The Amsterdam Congress reaffirms the resolutions adopted at the international socialist congresses held in Paris in 1889, in Brussels 1891, in Zurich 1893, and Paris in 1900 [see pages 25, 33–34, 43–44, and 78], and invites all the socialist parties and trade unions of all countries to organize energetically the working-class demonstrations of the First of May, in order to demand the institution of the legal eight-hour day, and to maintain the interests of the working-class and the cause of universal peace.

But this demonstration can be most effective only by the suspension of work on the First of May.

The Congress therefore urges it upon all proletarian organizations, as a duty, to strive to secure the complete stoppage of work on May First, wherever that can be done without injury to working-class interests.

***

WORKERS' INSURANCE

Commission resolution presented to the congress by Hermann Molkenbuhr on behalf of the German delegation.

Whereas the laborers, under capitalist society, receive a wage scarcely sufficient to cover the most pressing necessities of life during the time they are working, while they are destined to poverty and misery once they are prevented from utilizing their labor power, whether by illness, accident, impaired health, old age, or lockouts, or in the case of women, when they are prevented from working by pregnancy or maternity; and

Whereas every man has the right to live and society has an evident interest in conserving his labor power, it is necessary to establish institutions designed to obviate the misery of the laborers and to prevent the loss of labor power caused by it:

The laborers of all countries ought, therefore, to demand insurance laws by means of which they may obtain the right to receive sufficient assistance during the time when it is impossible for them to avail themselves of their own labor power by reason of illness, accident, failing health, old age, pregnancy, maternity, or lockouts.

The laborers should demand that the institutions for their insurance be put under the control of the insured themselves, and that the same conditions be accorded for the [native-born] laborers of the country and for foreigners of all nations [immigrant workers].

* * *

TRUSTS

Commission resolution presented by F. M. Wibaut, as amended by the congress, and approved by majority vote.

Trusts, in their complete development, eliminate competition among the masters of production. They gradually develop from loose associations of independent capitalists into gigantic and solidly organized corporations, national or even international, often leading to practical monopoly over various industries. They are the inevitable outcome of competition under a system of production by wage labor for capitalist profit. In these bodies, the great capitalists of all countries and of all industries are rapidly being welded into a compact unit on a basis of common material interest. Thus the conflict between the capitalists and working classes becomes ever sharper. Production is regulated, diminishing waste and increasing the productive power of labor. But the whole benefit goes to the capitalists, and the exploitation of labor is intensified.

In view of these facts and of the further fact that experience has amply proven the futility of antitrust legislation on the basis of our system of capitalist property and profit, the International Socialist Congress reaffirms and emphasizes the conclusions of the Paris Congress [see pages 79–80] to the following effect:

1. That the socialist parties in all countries ought to refrain from participation in any attempt to prevent the formation of trusts or to restrain their growth, regarding such attempts as always futile and often reactionary.

2. That the efforts of the socialist parties should be directed to establishing public ownership of all the means of production on a basis of public utility, eliminating profit. The method of effecting this socialization and the order in which it comes into effect will be determined by our power at the time of action and by the nature of the industries trustified.

3. Against the growing danger that threatens their economic organization through this solidification of capitalist forces, the workers of the world must set their organized power, united nationally and internationally, as their only weapon against capitalist oppression and the only means of overturning the capitalist system and establishing socialism.

* * *

COLONIAL POLICY

Commission resolution, signed by Louis de Brouckère, Hendrick Van Kol, and Alexandre Bracke, and adopted by the congress. Prior to the congress, the Dutch party had submitted a resolution, presumably drafted by Van Kol, which openly proclaimed a policy of "socialist colonialism." (See pages 153–55.) That call is not included in the resolution below, although point 5 does open the door to the idea of colonialism's "civilizing mission."

That this Congress, considering the ever-more-costly capitalist exploitation of an ever-extended colonial territory—exploitation not regulated and not restrained, which wastes capitals and natural riches, exposes the colonial populations to the most cruel, most terrible, and often the bloodiest oppression, and serves only to aggravate the misery of the proletariat;

Mindful of the resolution of the Paris Congress (1900) on the colonial question and imperialist policy [see page 72];

Declares that it is the duty of the national socialist parties and of the parliamentary groups:

1. To oppose without any compromise every imperialist or protectionist measure, every colonial expedition, and all military expenses for the colonies.

2. To fight every monopoly, every concession of vast territories, to prevent the wealth of the colonial territory from being appropriated by the all-powerful capitalists.

3. To denounce incessantly the deeds of oppression of which the natives are the victims, to obtain for them the most efficacious measures of protection against military acts of cruelty or capitalist exploitation, to prevent them from being robbed of their possessions, either by violence or by deceit.

4. To propose or to favor all that is conducive to the amelioration of the natives' conditions of life, public works, hygienic measures, schools, etc.; to do their utmost to withdraw them from the influence of the missionaries.

5. To claim for the natives that liberty and autonomy, compatible with their state of development, bearing in mind that the complete emancipation of the colonies is the object to pursue.

6. To try to bring the control of international policy—which, as the natural consequence of the capitalist system, is more and more influenced by financial gangs—under parliamentary control.

* * *

ON BRITISH INDIA

Motion read out by Samuel George Hobson of the British Fabian Society, and at least partially drafted by Henry Hyndman. Although asserting the right of colonial conquest and incorporating a "socialist colonialism" perspective, the motion was nevertheless adopted unanimously, without debate.

Resolved:

That this Congress, while recognizing the right of the inhabitants of civilized countries to settle in regions where the people are in lower stages of development, protests against and condemns, and urges all socialists to work to overthrow the capitalist system of conquering colonization under the capitalist regime of today. The results of this system are seen in the universal oppression by the most civilized nations of Europe—France, Germany, Holland, Belgium, England—of nations who come under their rule in Africa, Asia, and elsewhere. England is only the largest and most successful of such depredating nationalities. But the results in the case of British India are so much greater and more terrible than elsewhere.

That this meeting of the delegates of the workers of the civilized world, having heard from the representatives both of England and of India how British rule—by unceasingly and ever-increasingly plundering and drawing away the resources of the people, deliberately causes extreme impoverishment, and creates famines, plagues, and starvation on an ever-increasing scale for upwards of 200,000,000 of people in British territory in India—calls upon the workers of Great Britain to enforce upon their government the abandonment of the present nefarious and dishonorable system, and the establishment of self-government in the best form practicable by the Indians themselves (under British paramountcy).

* * *

SUPPORT FOR MINERS OF COLORADO

Adopted upon a motion by Keir Hardie and Herbert Burrows.

That this International Congress expresses its sincere sympathy with the locked-out trade union miners of Colorado, America, and most emphatically condemns the brutal outrages committed on them by the state authorities acting in the interests of the capitalist class, who have employed soldiers and armed police to break up the workers' organization, to arrest men and women and deport them for no cause except their membership of or sympathy with the miners' union, to enter and demolish homes and generally to crush by the use of armed force the peaceful attempt of the workers to ameliorate their position by combination and organization.[3]

* * *

SOLIDARITY WITH ITALIAN PRISONERS

Adopted upon a motion by Enrico Ferri.

The Congress expresses its solidarity sympathy for the work of the Comité, which organizes in Italy an agitation to realize the release of those who are condemned for the revolts of 1898 and who are still in prison—ardently wishing that they should be set at liberty.[4]

* * *

UNIVERSAL WOMEN'S SUFFRAGE

Adopted upon a motion by the German delegation.

In the struggles that the proletariat wages for the conquest of universal, equal, direct, and secret suffrage to parliament and municipal councils, socialist parties must put forward the demand for women's suffrage. This demand must be maintained as a principle in agitation and defended energetically.

* * *

ON HUNGARY

Adopted upon a motion read by Victor Serwy.

The International Socialist Congress of Amsterdam of 1904, basing itself, firstly, on written reports, and secondly, knowing of the shameful political and social conditions of Hungary, condemns the Hungarian ruling classes and their government due to their vile conduct toward the emancipation of the working class, and expresses its active sympathy for the conscious socialists in Hungary.[5]

* * *

THE RUSSO-JAPANESE WAR

Motion proposed by the French Socialist Party, adopted unanimously.

The Congress:

Considering that the agreement and concerted action of working people and socialists of all countries is the essential guarantee of international peace;

At a moment when tsarism is confronted simultaneously by war and by revolution:

Sends its fraternal greetings to Japanese and Russian proletarians, being massacred by the crimes of capitalism and its governments.[6]

And urges socialists and workers of all countries, guardians of international peace, to oppose by every means any extension of the war.

* * *

ANTI-SEMITIC PERSECUTION IN RUSSIA

Resolution submitted by August Bebel, Karl Hjalmar Branting, Eduard Bernstein, Hendrick Van Kol, Keir Hardie, and Edward Anseele. While the published proceedings in both German and French indicate that the resolution was adopted and greeted by prolonged applause,[7] the text itself is not found in the official record. The text of the resolution printed here appeared in the Yiddish-language newspaper of the Jewish Workers Bund.[8]

Millions of Russian Jews are being forced, through extreme government statutes, to live in the Pale of Settlement.[9] By these terrible means Jews are thus oppressed in their struggle to make a living, such that each year thousands of them are thrown into physical and moral ruin, according to the opinion of the Russian intelligentsia.

In order to divert the Russian people's attention away from the robbery and oppression they themselves face at the hands of the tsarist regime everywhere in the life of the country, the Russian government, from time to time, calls for pogroms against Jews, as evidenced by the savage Kishinev bloodbath, marshaled by Von Plehve, in order to snuff out and repress the dissemination of the ideas of socialism, which had in recent years begun to take deep root among Jewish workers of Lithuania, Poland, and Russia.[10]

Taking this into consideration, the International Socialist Congress in Amsterdam upholds its proud traditions and protests, in the name of freedom, the immoral hatred and unjust treatment of Russian Jews. We express our full and total sympathy with our Jewish comrades in Poland, Lithuania, and Russia—who are fighting for the realization of socialism in Russia—as well as our condemnation of all the other persecutions perpetrated by the "Paternal" Russian Government.

* * *

SUPPORT FOR RUSSIAN PROLETARIAT

Adopted upon a motion by Henriette Roland-Holst.

The Congress, in light of the innumerable difficulties that the proletariat of Russia encounters on the road to its liberation, along with the unheard-of sacrifices imposed on it, salutes the heroic proletarians who fight in fraternal unity without distinction of nationality, under the glorious banner of international socialism, against the yoke of absolutism and for the conquest of political liberties, and sends assurance of its deepest admiration and sympathy.

The Congress declares to the proletariat of Russia that the workers of the entire world are on their side in the struggle against absolutism, and that, in fighting for its own deliverance, it fights at the same time for the emancipation of the world proletariat.

7.

Stuttgart Congress, August 18–24, 1907

The Stuttgart Congress of 1907, attended by 884 delegates from 25 countries, took place as interimperialist rivalries and colonial wars continued to shape world politics. The congress was also the first international socialist congress since the Russian Revolution of 1905. That event, which extended into early 1907, was the first major revolutionary uprising in Europe since the Paris Commune of 1871. It inspired and energized the working-class movement of the entire world, particularly left-wing forces within the parties of the Second International, leading to growing polarization in the world movement.

These international events shaped the debates at Stuttgart, in which the growing divergence between the revolutionary and opportunist trends within the Second International was unusually sharp and clear-cut.

There were important debates at the Stuttgart Congress around five issues:

1. War and militarism.

Four resolutions were presented to the congress. The main one, put forward by August Bebel on behalf of the German Social Democratic Party (SPD), was largely a restatement of resolutions adopted at previous congresses, condemning capitalist militarism in a general sense. But it lacked any concrete statement regarding action to be taken by the working class in response to the threat of war. A second resolution, put forward by Jean Jaurès and Édouard Vaillant for the majority of the French delegation, restated the position the French had been putting forward for years on the need to meet war threats with a general strike. A more extreme version of this view was presented in a resolution by

Gustave Hervé, who called for meeting war threats with insurrection and military disobedience. The final resolution, put forward by Jules Guesde for the French minority, rejected any special antiwar measures apart from the general fight for socialism.

A debate over these resolutions took place in the congress commission on war and international conflicts. A subcommission was then established to prepare a draft for the congress itself. In this subcommission, Rosa Luxemburg submitted a series of amendments to Bebel's resolution prepared by her, V. I. Lenin, and Julius Martov. These amendments sharpened the Bebel resolution considerably, spelling out the need not just for the working class to oppose these wars formally but also to take concrete action against them, and to do so in such a way as to advance the perspective of proletarian revolution. These amendments were incorporated into Bebel's draft, and the amended resolution was then unanimously adopted by the commission and presented to the congress plenary, where it was also adopted unanimously. (For a version of the resolution that highlights the Luxemburg-Lenin-Martov amendments, see the appendix, pages 157–59.)

2. Immigration and emigration.

A sharp debate occurred within the commission taking up the question of emigration and immigration of workers. Morris Hillquit, who defended a resolution submitted by the Socialist Party of America, focused on "capitalism's importation of foreign labor cheaper than that of native-born workers." He went on to say,

> This threatens the native-born with dangerous competition and usually provides a pool of unconscious strikebreakers. Chinese and Japanese workers play that role today, as does the yellow race in general. While we have absolutely no racial prejudices against the Chinese, we must frankly tell you that they cannot be organized. Only a people well advanced in its historical development, such as the Belgians and Italians in France, can be organized for the class struggle. The Chinese have lagged too far behind to be organized.[1]

Hillquit's anti-immigrant and prejudiced views were answered heatedly by a number of speakers, who expressed the traditional socialist stance opposing immigration restrictions and welcoming immigrant workers as allies in the struggle. The US SP resolution on immigration was rejected in the commission and by the congress plenary, although the exact vote totals are not recorded in the proceedings. (For the text of the Socialist Party of America resolution, see the appendix, pages 156–57.)

3. Colonialism.

The congress commission taking up the colonial question adopted a resolution put forward by Hendrick Van Kol, in line with the "socialist colonialism" remark he had made at the Amsterdam Congress four years earlier. This pro-colonialism view was hotly contested in the commission, but Van Kol's resolution was adopted there with 18 votes in favor against 10 for the commission minority.

When the congress plenary took up the question, however, the vote was reversed. There the colonialism resolution of the commission minority was approved by 127 votes against 108, with 10 abstentions.[2] The traditional socialist condemnation of bourgeois colonial policy was therefore adopted—but by a surprisingly narrow margin. (For the text of Van Kol's commission majority resolution, see the appendix, page 155.)

4. The relations between trade unions and political parties.

A debate occurred at the Stuttgart Congress over whether trade unions should be neutral on the question of working-class political power. Within the commission, the main resolution taking up this question, presented by Louis de Brouckère for the Belgian delegation, reaffirmed the traditional view of the Second International opposing the "neutrality" principle and stressing the need for permanent and close contact between trade unions and socialist parties. A slightly different resolution was presented by Max Beer for the Austrian delegation, which put more stress on the need for a strict division of labor between the two. Eventually a combined Belgian-Austrian compromise resolution was accepted by the commission. The majority of the French delegation opposed this resolution and defended the traditional syndicalist view concerning the absolute autonomy of unions and parties.

The Belgian-Austrian resolution was adopted by the commission with 7 votes against. In the congress plenary, it was adopted by a vote of 222 ½ to 18 ½ against, with 4 abstentions.

5. Women's suffrage.

On the eve of the Stuttgart Congress, the First International Socialist Women's Conference was held, under the leadership and guidance of Clara Zetkin. A debate occurred there on the question of women's suffrage. At the time, women could not vote in most countries, and movements for women's right to vote were beginning to have an impact on politics in many places.

The socialist movement's longstanding position was to unconditionally support women's right to vote. In opposition to this stance, at the International Socialist Women's Conference, the British Independent Labour Party and Fabian Society put forward a call to support limited women's suffrage, with property qualifications. Additionally, the Austrian delegates—who were in the midst of a struggle for universal male suffrage—presented the view that in some cases, for practical reasons, it was permissible to back off from supporting women's suffrage in order to campaign for universal male suffrage.

A resolution calling for no compromise on this question, put forward by Zetkin on behalf of the German SPD delegation to the Socialist Women's Conference, was approved 47 to 11 at that conference. Zetkin's resolution was then brought into the Second International congress and adopted.

RULES FOR INTERNATIONAL CONGRESSES AND
THE INTERNATIONAL SOCIALIST BUREAU

The following rules were approved by the congress.

I

Those admitted to international socialist congresses are:

A. All associations that adhere to the essential principles of socialism: socialization of the means of production and exchange; international union and actions of the workers; conquest of public powers by the proletarians, organized as a class-party.

B. All labor organizations that accept the principles of class struggle and recognize the necessity of political action (legislative and parliamentary) but do not participate directly in the political movement (international congress held in Paris 1900).

II

A. The parties and organizations of each country or nation constitute one section that itself decides upon the admission of all other parties and organizations of the countries or nations concerned.

The parties and organizations not admitted by the section have the right of appeal to the International Socialist Bureau, which decides in the last resort.

B. The National Committee of each section, or in default of it the secretary of each affiliated party, will transmit to the socialist groups and other affiliated organizations the invitations to attend the international congress and the resolutions adopted by the International Socialist Bureau.

The texts of all resolutions must be in possession of the Bureau fully three months before the date fixed for the meeting of the international congress and be distributed a month after receipt.

No new resolution whatever will be accepted, distributed, or discussed unless it is in accordance with this rule, except matters in which urgency is admitted. The International Socialist Bureau is alone competent to decide on the question of urgency, but the amendments or resolutions must be drawn up and submitted to the International Bureau, which will decide if the amendments are acceptable or not, and are not attempts to put forward new resolutions in the shape of amendments.

III

The manner of voting at international congresses is established by the following rules:

A. Voting is per head, and per national sections, when three represented nations demand it.

B. Each section will have a number of votes varying from two to twenty, according to a list that will be issued for the first time by the International Socialist Bureau 1906–07. This list will be periodically revised when the circumstances require it.

C. The division of votes for each nation will be fixed:

(a) According to the number of paying members, taking into consideration the number of inhabitants;

(b) According to the importance of the nationality;

(c) According to the strength of the trade union, cooperative, and socialist organizations;

(d) According to the political power of the socialist party or parties.

The affiliation of the paying members will be proved by such documents or accounts as the Bureau may ask for.

D. The sections divide the votes that have been allotted to them. If the whole of the parties or organizations forming the section cannot agree on the division of votes, it will be decided by the International Socialist Bureau.

IV

An International Socialist Bureau, based on the representation of the national sections of the international congress, shall continue their functions. Each section can send two delegates to the Bureau. The delegates may be replaced by substitutes, mandated by the affiliated parties. The national secretaries of the Interparliamentary Commission will act as assistant delegates and may, in this capacity, attend the meetings of the International Socialist Bureau.

V

The Bureau has a permanent secretary, whose functions were determined by the Paris Congress in 1900 [see page 68]. The secretary has his residence in Brussels and the Belgian delegation [Belgian ISB members] shall act as the Executive Committee.

VI

The contributions of each affiliated party shall fall due each year in January, according to a scale established periodically by the Bureau.

* * *

STATUTES OF THE INTERPARLIAMENTARY COMMISSION

These statutes were adopted at a meeting of the Interparliamentary Committee held August 17, 1907, on the eve of the congress. They were then approved by the congress itself.

ARTICLE 1. The Interparliamentary Committee (IC) was founded on August 20, 1904, by the Amsterdam International Socialist Congress, pursuant to the following resolutions of the international congresses of London and Paris:

> The International Socialist Committee will require socialist members of parliament in each country to form a special interparliamentary commission to facilitate common action on the big international political and economic questions. This commission will be assisted by the International Socialist Bureau. (Paris Congress, 1900). [See pages 68–69.]
>
> An Interparliamentary Conference has been established, composed of one delegate of each nationality. Its object is the unification of parliamentary work in all countries. (Communications to be addressed to Édouard Vaillant.) (London Congress, 1896)[3]

ARTICLE 2. The year begins on September 1, and closes on August 31.

ARTICLE 3. Members of the IC are:

The parliamentary groups of the parties affiliated to the International Socialist Bureau and having applied for membership in the IC. When such application is made, the parliamentary group appoints one of its members as secretary-correspondent. Each parliamentary group is considered as representing the party to which it belongs.

ARTICLE 4. The office of secretary of the IC will be filled by the secretary of the ISB.

ARTICLE 5. Every parliamentary group must, through correspondence and documents, keep the IC informed of the legislative activity of their party.

The IC is responsible, to the degree possible, for satisfying every request for information by sending documents and materials.

A. For this purpose, the IC must respond to requests, through both summary notes and special packets of material, on the question at hand, giving dates and texts of laws passed.

B. By sending out laws drafted by one parliamentary group on an issue, the IC will put the other parliamentary groups in a position to present similar drafts based on the conditions specific to their countries, but as much as possible simultaneously and in accordance with these draft laws.

C. The parliamentary fractions affiliated to the Interparliamentary Commission will send to the secretariat the texts and materials concerning laws drafted on their initiative. The Interparliamentary Commission will publish them and make all the documents available to other affiliated fractions on the various questions of labor legislation. The Interparliamentary Commission, for its part, has the right to request information from an affiliated fraction concerning current legislative issues.

ARTICLE 6. The finances of the IC consist of the obligatory and voluntary contributions of its members. The obligatory contribution of each party is 5 francs (4 shillings) for every deputy it sends to parliament.

The sum total of annual contributions—dues for parliamentarians of affiliated sections or parties—is payable at the same time as the dues of sections and parties to the International Socialist Bureau.

ARTICLE 7. One ordinary assembly will be held every year, following the meeting of the Bureau, an assembly to which will be admitted all the members of the parliamentary groups affiliated to the IC.

This conference appoints the place where the next one will be held.

ARTICLE 8. There will also be extraordinary conferences, at which each parliamentary group may be represented by one or more delegates.

ARTICLE 9. Such an extraordinary conference is to be called when desired by five parliamentary groups.

Such an extraordinary assembly will be called, at the same time and place as the meeting of the International Socialist Bureau, as soon as secret or public events occasion fear of conflicts between governments and make war possible or probable, in order to arrange and discuss the common and combined means of action by labor and socialism to oppose and to prevent war.

ARTICLE 10. The International Socialist Bureau is entitled to be represented at every meeting of the IC, to take part in its discussions, to propose resolutions, and to a consultative vote.

The national secretaries of the IC will have the status of deputy delegates to the ISB, and in that capacity they may attend meetings of the Bureau.

ARTICLE 11. The voting system shall be similar to that adopted by the International Socialist Bureau.

ARTICLE 12. The rules, as also eventual modifications, shall only be valid when the International Socialist Bureau has approved of the same.

***

MILITARISM AND INTERNATIONAL CONFLICTS

Resolution of the First Commission, presented to the congress by Émile Vandervelde. The original draft was prepared by August Bebel. In the commission, a series of amendments presented jointly by Rosa Luxemburg, V. I. Lenin, and Julius Martov were adopted and incorporated in the text, which was then adopted by the congress. For a version of this resolution that highlights the Luxemburg–Lenin–Martov amendments, see the appendix, pages 157–59.

The Congress reaffirms the resolutions passed by previous international congresses against militarism and imperialism, and it again declares that the fight against militarism cannot be separated from the socialist class struggle as a whole.

Wars between capitalist states are as a rule the consequence of their competition in the world market, for every state is eager not only to preserve its markets but also to conquer new ones, principally by the subjugation of foreign nations and the confiscation of their lands. These wars are further engendered by the unceasing and ever-increasing armaments of militarism, which is one of the principal instruments for maintaining bourgeois class rule and for subjugating the working classes politically and economically.

The outbreak of wars is further promoted by the national prejudices systematically cultivated in the interest of the ruling classes, in order to divert the masses of the proletariat from their class duties and international solidarity.

Wars are therefore essential to capitalism; they will not cease until the capitalist system has been done away with, or until the sacrifices in men and money required by the technical development of the military system and the rejection of the armaments race have become so great as to compel the nations to abandon this system.

The working class especially, from which the soldiers are chiefly recruited, and which has to bear the greater part of the financial burdens, is by nature opposed to war, because war is irreconcilable with its aim: the creation of a new economic system founded on a socialist basis and realizing the solidarity of nations.

The Congress therefore considers it to be the duty of the working class, and especially of its parliamentary representatives, to fight with all their might against military and naval armaments, not to grant any money for such purposes, pointing out at the same time the class character of bourgeois society and the real motives for maintaining national antagonisms, and further, to imbue working-class youth with the socialist spirit of universal brotherhood and developing their class consciousness.

The Congress considers that the democratic organization of national defense, by replacing the standing army with the armed people, will prove an effective means for making aggressive wars impossible, and for overcoming national antagonisms.

The International cannot lay down rigid formulas for action by the working class against militarism, as this action must of necessity differ according to the time and conditions of the various national parties. But it is the duty of the International to intensify and coordinate, as much as possible, the efforts of the working class against militarism and war.

In fact, since the Brussels Congress [of 1891], the proletariat in its untiring fight against militarism, by refusing to grant the expenses for military and naval armaments, by democratizing the army, has had recourse, with increasing vigor and success, to the most varied methods of action in order to prevent the outbreak of wars, or to end them, or to make use of the social convulsions caused by war for the emancipation of the working class: as for instance the understanding arrived at between the British and French trade unions after the Fashoda crisis, which served to assure peace and to reestablish friendly relations between Britain and France;[4] the action of the socialist parties in the German and French parliaments during the Morocco crisis: the public demonstrations organized for the same purpose by the French and German socialists;[5] the common action of the Austrian and Italian socialists who met at Trieste in order to ward off a conflict between the two states;[6] further, the vigorous intervention of the socialist workers of Sweden in order to prevent an attack against Norway;[7] and lastly, the heroic sacrifices and fights of the masses of socialist workers and peasants of Russia and Poland rising against the war provoked by the government of the tsar, in order to put an end to it and to make use of the crisis for the emancipation of their country and of the working class.[8] All these efforts show the growing power of the proletariat and its increasing desire to maintain peace by its energetic intervention.

The action of the working classes will be the more successful, the more the mind of the people has been prepared by an unceasing propaganda, and the more the labor parties of the different countries have been spurred on and coordinated by the International.

The Congress further expresses its conviction that under the pressure exerted by the proletariat, the practice of honest arbitration in all disputes will replace the futile attempts of the bourgeois governments, and that in this way the people will be assured of the benefits of universal disarmament, which will allow the enormous resources of energy and money, wasted by armaments and wars, to be applied to the progress of civilization.

In case of war being imminent, the working class and its parliamentary representatives in the countries concerned shall be bound, with the assistance of the International Socialist Bureau, to do all they can to prevent the outbreak of war, using for this purpose the means that appear to them the most effective, and which must naturally vary according to the acuteness of the class struggle and to the general political conditions.

In case war should break out notwithstanding, they shall be bound to intervene for its speedy termination, and to employ all their forces to utilize the economic and political crisis created by the war in order to rouse the masses of the people and thereby hasten the downfall of capitalist class rule.

* * *

THE RELATIONS BETWEEN TRADE UNIONS AND SOCIALIST PARTIES

Resolution of the Second Commission, presented to the congress by Max Beer. It was adopted in the plenary by a vote of 222 ½ to 18 ½ against, with 4 abstentions.

I

To free the proletariat completely from the bonds of intellectual, political, and economic serfdom, the political and economic struggle are alike necessary. If the activity of the Socialist Party is exercised more especially in the domain of the political struggle of the proletariat, that of the unions displays itself in the domain of the economic struggle of the workers. The unions and the party have therefore an equally important task to perform in the struggle for proletarian emancipation. Each of the two organizations has its distinct domain, defined by its nature and within whose borders it should enjoy independent control of its line of action. But there is an ever-widening domain in the proletarian struggle of the classes in which they can only reap advantages by concerted action and by cooperation between the party and trade unions.

As a consequence, the proletarian struggle will be carried on more successfully and with more important results if the relations between the unions and the party are strengthened without infringing the necessary unity of the trade unions.

The Congress declares that it is in the interest of the working class in every country that close and permanent relations should be established between the unions and the party.

It is the duty of the party and of the trade unions to render moral support the one to the other, and to make use only of those means that may help advance the emancipation of the proletariat. When divergent opinions arise between the two organizations as to the suitability of certain tactics, they should arrive at an agreement through discussion.

The unions will not fully perform their duty in the struggle for the emancipation of the workers unless a thoroughly socialist spirit inspires their policy. It is the duty of the party to help the unions in their work of raising the workers and of ameliorating their social conditions. In its parliamentary action the party must vigorously support the demands of the unions.

The Congress declares that the development of the capitalist system of production, the increased concentration of the means of production, the growing alliances of employers, and the increasing dependence of particular trades upon the totality of bourgeois society would reduce trade unions to impotency if, concerning themselves about nothing more than trade interests, they took their stand on corporate selfishness and admitted the theory of harmony of interests between labor and capital.

The Congress is of the opinion that the unions will be able more successfully to carry on their struggle against exploitation and oppression, in proportion as their organization is more unified, as their benefit system is improved, as the funds necessary for their struggle are better supplied, and as their members gain a clearer conception of economic relations and conditions and are inspired by the socialist ideal with greater enthusiasm and devotion.

II

The Congress urges all the trade unions that accept the conditions laid down by the Brussels conference of 1899 and ratified by the Paris Congress of 1900,[9] to be represented at the international congress and to maintain relations with the International Socialist Bureau. It charges the latter to enter into relations with the International Secretariat of Trade Unions at Berlin so as to exchange information respecting working-class organization and the workers' movement.[10]

III

The Congress directs the International Bureau to collect all documents that may facilitate the study of the relations between trade organizations and the socialist parties in all countries and to present a report on the subject to the next congress.

* * *

THE COLONIAL QUESTION

The Third Commission, dealing with the colonial question, was the scene of heated debate. It approved, by a vote of 18 to 10, a resolution drafted by Hendrick Van Kol that endorsed the "socialist colonialism" perspective Van Kol had been putting forward. A minority of the commission opposed to this perspective submitted a counterresolution, proposed by Georg Ledebour, Emmanuel Wurm, Henri de la Porte, Alexandre Bracke, and Karski (Julian Marchlewski). When the rival commission resolutions were submitted to the congress plenary, however, the Van Kol resolution was rejected, and the commission minority's resolution, below, was adopted by a vote of 127 to 108, with 10 abstentions. For the text of Van Kol's Colonial Commission majority resolution, see the appendix, page 155.

The Congress is of the opinion that capitalist colonial policy, by its very nature, must lead to enslavement and compulsory labor or to the extermination of the native population of the colonial territories.

The civilizing mission, to which capitalist society appeals, serves only as a cover for a burning passion for conquest and exploitation. Only with the achievement of the socialist society will it be possible for all peoples to develop themselves to a complete civilization.

Capitalist colonial policy, instead of increasing the productive forces, by the very fact that it enslaves and pauperizes the natives, as well as the damage that it inflicts by war, destroys the natural riches of the countries in which it plants its methods. It renders slower or hinders thereby the very development of commerce and of the sale of the industrial products of the civilized states.

The Congress condemns the barbaric methods of capitalist colonization and demands in the interest of the development of the productive forces, a policy that guarantees the peaceful development of civilization and places the natural riches at the disposal of the entire humanity.

In reaffirmation of the Paris (1900) and Amsterdam (1904) resolutions [see pages 72 and 88–89], the Congress repudiates colonization, as at present carried on, since being of a capitalist character, it has no other aim but to conquer new countries, and to subjugate their populations in order to exploit them mercilessly for the benefit of an insignificant minority, while increasing the burden on the proletariat at home.

The Congress, as an enemy of all exploitation of man by man, and the defender of all oppressed without distinction of race, condemns this policy of robbery and conquest, this shameless application of the right of the strong trampling underfoot the rights of the vanquished races; and further states that this colonial system increases the danger of international complications and war, thus making heavier the financial burdens for navy and army.

From the financial point of view, the colonial expenses—both those that arise from imperialism and those that are necessary to further the economic evolution of the colonies—must be borne by those who profit from the spoliation of the colonies and derive their wealth therefrom.

The Congress declares finally that it is the duty of the socialist members of parliament to oppose without compromise in their respective parliaments the regime of exploitation and serfdom that prevails in all colonies of today, to exact reforms for the amelioration of the condition of the natives, to safeguard their rights by preventing their exploitation and enslavement, and to work with every means at their disposal for the education of these races to independence.

* * *

IMMIGRATION AND EMIGRATION OF WORKERS

Resolution of the Fourth Commission, presented to the congress by Wilhelm Ellenbogen. A debate occurred in the commission, as Morris Hillquit from the Socialist Party of America raised the need for restrictions on Chinese and Japanese immigration. That position was rejected by the commission majority. For the US SP resolution on immigration, see the appendix, pages 156–57.

The Congress declares:

Immigration and emigration of workers are phenomena as inseparable from the substance of capitalism as unemployment, overproduction, and underconsumption of the workers; they are frequently one of the means to reduce the share of the workers in the product of labor, and at times they assume abnormal dimensions through political, religious, and national persecutions.

The Congress does not consider exceptional measures of any kind, economic or political, [to be] the means for removing any danger that may arise to the working class from immigration and emigration, since such measures are fruitless and reactionary: especially not the restriction of the freedom of migration and the exclusion of foreign nations and races.

At the same time, the Congress declares it to be the duty of organized workers to protect themselves against the lowering of their standard of living, which frequently results from the mass import of unorganized workers. The Congress declares it to be their duty to prevent the import and export of strikebreakers.

The Congress recognizes the difficulties that in many cases confront the workers of the countries of a more advanced stage of capitalist development through the mass immigration of unorganized workers accustomed to a lower standard of living and coming from countries of prevalently agricultural and domestic civilization, and also the dangers that confront them from certain forms of immigration.

But the Congress sees no proper solution of these difficulties in the exclusion of definite nations or races from immigration, a policy that is besides in conflict with the principle of proletarian solidarity.

The Congress, therefore, recommends the following measures:

I. *For the countries of immigration:*

1. Prohibition of the export and import of such workers who have entered into a contract that deprives them of the liberty to dispose of their labor power and wages.

2. Legislation shortening the workday, fixing a minimum wage, regulating the sweating system [sweatshops] and house industry, and providing for strict supervision of sanitary and dwelling conditions.

3. Abolition of all restrictions that exclude definite nationalities or races from the right of sojourn in the country and from the political and economic rights of the natives, or make the acquisition of these rights more difficult for them. It also demands the greatest latitude in the laws of naturalization.

4. For the trade unions of all countries, the following principles shall have universal application in connection with it:

(a) Unrestricted admission of immigrant workers to the trade unions of all countries.

(b) Facilitating the admission of members by means of fixing reasonable admission fees.

(c) Free transfer from the organizations of one country to those of the other upon the discharge of the membership obligations towards the former organization.

(d) The making of international trade union agreements for the purpose of regulating these questions in a definite and proper manner, and enabling the realization of these principles on an international scale.

5. Support of the trade unions of those countries from which the immigration is chiefly recruited.

II. *For the country of emigration:*

1. Active propaganda for trade unionism.

2. Enlightenment of the workers and the public at large on the true conditions of labor in the countries of immigration.

3. Concerted action on the part of the trade unions of all countries in all matters of labor immigration and emigration.

4. In view of the fact that emigration of workers is often artificially stimulated by railway and steamship companies, land speculators, and

other swindling concerns through false and lying promises to workers, the Congress demands:

Control of the steamship agencies and emigration bureaus, and legal and administrative measures against them, in order to prevent emigration from being abused in the interests of such capitalist concerns.

III. Regulation of the system of transportation, especially on ships. Employment of inspectors with discretionary power over who should be selected by the organized workers of the countries of emigration and immigration. Protection for the newly arrived immigrants, in order that they may not become the victims of capitalist exploiters.

In view of the fact that the transport of emigrants can only be regulated on an international basis, the Congress directs the International Socialist Bureau to prepare suggestions for the regulation of this question, which shall deal with the conditions, arrangements, and supplies of the ships, the air space to be allowed for each passenger as a minimum, and shall lay special stress that the individual emigrants contract for their passage directly with the transportation companies and without intervention of middlemen. These suggestions shall be communicated to the various socialist parties for the purpose of legislative application, and adaptation, as well as for the purposes of propaganda.

* * *

WOMEN'S SUFFRAGE

Resolution of the Fifth Commission, presented to the congress plenary by Clara Zetkin. This resolution was based on the one adopted by the First International Socialist Women's Conference, which had taken place on the eve of the international congress. It was then approved by the Second International's congress with one dissenting vote, from the Fabian Society.

The Congress greets with the utmost pleasure the First International Socialist Women's Conference, and expresses its entire solidarity with the demands concerning women's suffrage put forward by it.

The Socialist Party repudiates limited women's suffrage as an adulteration and a caricature of the principle of political equality of the female sex. It fights for the sole living, concrete expression of this principle: namely, universal women's suffrage, which should belong to all women of age and not be conditioned by property, taxation, education, or any other qualification that would exclude members of the laboring classes from the enjoyment of this right. The socialist women shall not carry on this struggle for complete equality of right of vote in alliance with the bourgeois feminists, but in common with the socialist parties, which insist upon women's suffrage as one of the fundamental and most important reforms for the full democratization of the political franchise in general.

It is the duty of the socialist parties of all countries to agitate strenuously for the introduction of universal women's suffrage. Hence, the agitation for the democratization of the franchise to the legislative and administrative bodies, both national and local, must also embrace women's suffrage and must insist upon it, whether it be carried out in parliament or elsewhere. In those countries where the democratization of manhood suffrage has already gone sufficiently far, or is completely realized, the socialist parties must raise a campaign in favor of universal women's suffrage, and in connection with it, of course, put forward all those demands that we have yet to realize in the interest of the full civil rights of the male portion of the proletariat.

Although the International Socialist Congress cannot dictate to any country a particular time at which a suffrage campaign should be commenced, it nevertheless declares that when such a campaign is instituted in any country, it should proceed on the general Social Democratic lines of universal adult suffrage without distinction, and nothing less.

* * *

ON ROMANIA

Resolution proposed by Romanian delegates and adopted unanimously.

The International Socialist Bureau has been informed by the Romanian delegation that the Romanian government has adopted a policy of extermination towards the people of the town and country districts.[11]

After having killed thousands and thousands of peasants who had been forced to make an unhappy revolt by the system of unlimited exploitation and oppression, the government is now attacking the working-class organizations, the trade unions and socialist societies, and strives to outlaw them by wholesale arrests and condemnations to exile. It is not only foreign workers who are expelled from the country but also an entire category of Romanian citizens, the Jewish workmen of Romania who are not considered subjects of any other country; now on foreign soil, they therefore have no national protection and are rejected from these foreign countries.

This odious persecution is contrary to all the laws of humanity and in opposition to the international obligations of the Romanian government. Finally, this policy of savage persecution constitutes an act of defiance against the international proletariat, whose interests are identical.

The Bureau therefore proposes that the Congress should express, at one and the same time, its good wishes and every encouragement for the Romanian proletariat in its struggle to acquire its rights; and also protests indignantly against the odious policy of the Romanian government.

At the same time, it urges the socialist deputies of the different parliaments to ask that the Romanian government fulfill its obligations toward the different categories of citizens of Romania, which international treaties have placed under its protection.

Further, the Congress recommends the workers of different countries not to accept the invitations made by the Romanian employers; for at the first sign of solidarity they may show towards their Romanian fellow workers, they will be piteously expelled from the country.

The Congress also calls upon the Romanian delegation to present a memorandum giving full details of cases submitted to the Bureau.

* * *

GREETINGS TO REVOLUTIONARIES OF RUSSIA

Adopted unanimously by the congress on a motion submitted by Henry Hyndman, Samuel George Hobson, Enrico Ferri, Amilcare Cipriani, Jules Guesde, Gustave Delory, Jean Jaurès, Édouard Vaillant, Victor Adler, Karl Kautsky, August Bebel, and Morris Hillquit.

The Congress holds that the Russian Revolution, although only just begun, is already a powerful factor in the international struggle of labor against capital, and it sends its fraternal greetings to the heroic combatants of the Russian working class of town and country.

* * *

ON MOROCCO

Resolution proposed by the French and Spanish delegations and adopted unanimously.

The Congress reiterates its decision with regard to colonial undertakings, as well as its condemnation of militarism.

It denounces before the world proletariat the current French-Spanish campaign in Morocco, which arises, as in all similar cases, from capitalism's financial speculations.[12]

It condemns this new example of the bourgeoisie's constant practice of shedding the blood of workers for its own benefit.

It urges socialist parties of all countries—and especially the working people of France and Spain—to undertake vigorous action to stop the Franco-Spanish expedition in Morocco, which threatens all of Europe with expanding international conflicts.

* * *

THE TRIAL OF THE AMERICAN MINERS

This resolution adopted by the congress was signed by A. M. Simons, Robert Hunter, Morris Hillquit, Algernon Lee, Frank Bohn, Jean Longuet, Amilcare Cipriani, Karl Kautsky, August Bebel, Paul Singer, Hendrick Van Kol, Camille Huysmans, Rosa Luxemburg, V. I. Lenin, Émile Vandervelde, Edward Anseele, Enrico Ferri, Peter Knudsen, H. M. Hyndman, Jean Jaurès, and Victor Adler.

The International Socialist Congress sends to William D. Haywood the salute of the socialist world, for the admirable struggle he has waged in the interests of the organized proletariat of the United States.[13]

The Congress condemns the effort by the mine owners in their goal of sentencing an innocent man for the services he has rendered to the cause of the organized proletariat.

The Congress views the illegal form of his arrest and trial, along with the systematic campaign of slander against him by the entire capitalist class and its government and press, as the expression of an increasingly brutal class policy and of its complete lack of tolerance and honor in all cases where their profits and their power are concerned.

The Congress, at the same time, salutes the proletarians and social-ists of the United States for the unanimity and enthusiasm with which they have responded to this attack. The conscious proletariat of Europe views the power of their solidarity action as a pledge and guarantee for the future, and it hopes that this same unanimity and solidarity of the American proletariat is maintained in its struggle for the definitive emancipation of labor.

8.

Copenhagen Congress, August 28–September 3, 1910

The Second International's Copenhagen Congress drew 896 delegates from twenty-three countries.

Since the previous congress, international tensions had continued to build, along with important struggles by working people in many countries. In line with this world situation, the question of international working-class solidarity was a major theme of the congress, with numerous resolutions and motions adopted.

One of the most substantial congress resolutions was on militarism and war. As the arms buildup in Europe continued, with growing war threats and new incidents that could potentially lead to conflict between the imperialist powers, calls were made for more aggressive commitments to antiwar action. Keir Hardie from Britain and Édouard Vaillant from France in particular pressed for a commitment to more vigorous antiwar action. Their resolution was defeated in the militarism commission, although Hardie and Vaillant did obtain a promise by the congress to study the matter and report on it at the next international congress. The resolution adopted by the congress largely restated the conclusions of the Stuttgart resolution on war and militarism.

The issue of cooperatives and the cooperative movement was one of the more contentious and significant issues at the congress.

During the late nineteenth and early twentieth centuries, cooperatives played a major part in the working-class movement as a whole. Millions of working people belonged to cooperatives, which made up a third wing of the workers' movement, alongside parties and trade unions. In the days before any type of government health insurance or most other social benefits, cooperatives played a big role in workers' lives and made it more possible for them to get involved in the broader struggle.

Two main lines were presented at the congress on this question: those who saw cooperatives as a weapon in the class struggle, and those who viewed cooperatives primarily as a model of the future socialist society, abstracted from the struggle of working people against capitalism. The resolution adopted largely reflected the first view, although there were points of unclarity in it. One of the participants in the congress commission on the question was V. I. Lenin, who submitted his own resolution to the commission (see the appendix, pages 159–60).

The Copenhagen Congress was important in another way, too.

At the congress, Lenin sought to build on the efforts begun at Stuttgart in 1907 to coalesce a left wing within the Second International. During the days of the congress, Lenin organized a meeting of left-wing delegates to try to coordinate their work and to increase international left-wing collaboration. Among the dozen or so who came to the meeting were Rosa Luxemburg, Jules Guesde, and Georgy Plekhanov.

THE UNEMPLOYMENT QUESTION

Resolution of the Commission on Labor Legislation and Unemployment (Fourth Commission), presented to the congress plenary by Adolf Braun and adopted by a large majority. The original draft was prepared by the French Socialist Party.

The Congress declares that unemployment is inseparable from the capitalist mode of production and will disappear only when capitalism disappears. So long as capitalist production forms the basis of society, palliative measures alone are possible.

This Congress demands the institution by public authorities, under the administration of working-class organizations, of general compulsory insurance against unemployment, the expenses of which shall be borne by the owners of the means of production.

The representatives of the workers most urgently demand from the public authorities:

1. Exact statistical registration of the unemployed.

2. The execution on a sufficient scale of important public works, where the unemployed shall be paid the trade union rate of wages.

3. In periods of industrial crisis, extraordinary subsidies to trade union unemployed funds.

4. No payment to an unemployed worker is to cause the loss of political rights.

5. Establishment of and subsidies to labor exchanges, in which all the liberties and interests of the workers are respected by cooperation with trade union employment bureaus.

6. Social laws for the regulation and reduction of hours of work.

7. Pending the realization by legislation on general and compulsory insurance, the public authorities should encourage unemployment benefit funds of trade unions by financial subsidies, these subsidies leaving complete autonomy to the trade union.

* * *

THE DEATH PENALTY

Presented by the Commission on Resolutions (Fifth Commission). The original draft had been submitted by the Social Democratic Party of Germany.

At the dawn of modern social evolution, bourgeois rationalism condemned the death penalty as a barbaric relic of the Middle Ages. The idea of the progress of humanity did not, for the revolutionary bourgeoisie, mean only empty phrases. As a consequence, its most eminent representatives in every country proclaimed a struggle by civilized humanity against this shameful institution, as nothing but legalized and systematic murder, committed in cold blood by one man against another.

Since then a profound change has taken place in relation to this question. The ever-increasing struggle between the bourgeoisie and the proletariat (which becomes daily more and more the center of public life of each country) has induced the degenerate bourgeoisie of our days to abandon the struggle against the death penalty, along with many other democratic and liberal measures. The ruling classes employ more and more the ignominious weapon of the death penalty, sometimes to fight against the decomposition of the capitalist order itself, and sometimes to forcibly suppress the proletariat fighting for its emancipation.

In Germany, and in many other countries that present themselves as civilized masters of science and art, the most brilliant bourgeois intellectuals have lately declared the death penalty to be necessary. Eminent representatives of modern criminal science have recently declared themselves in favor of essential modifications of the right of asylum, which especially in the case of Russian emigrants, would have the effect of restoring the death penalty, even in countries, where, as in Holland, it has been abolished for a long time. In the French republic, the parliament has voted against a measure abolishing the death penalty. In the United States of North America the bourgeoisie fights a militant proletariat with the death penalty. Only a short time ago, the never-to-be-forgotten victims of judicial murder in Chicago were hanged for having demanded the eight-hour day, and were very nearly followed by the execution of the representatives of the organized miners.[1] In Spain a worn-out and reactionary regime uses judicial murder as a weapon and a means of vengeance against the aspirations of the proletariat for emancipation. Finally in Russia, a country where the death penalty has long been abolished for common-law crimes, the executioner has been active all throughout the revolution of the working population, and especially since the victory of the counterrevolution. Thousands and thousands of persons are executed after a contemptible comedy of a military court-martial. A river of blood is spreading through the whole Russian Empire. All this is being done before the eyes of the civilized world, while the bourgeois intellectual representatives dare not offer any resistance, without refusing their moral complicity and their financial help to the executioner's regime. A large number of bourgeois intellectuals, who showed indignation at the execution of the freethinker Ferrer,[2] look on calmly while the Russian autocracy combats the proletarian revolution by wholesale massacres.

For this reason, the socialist proletariat is today the most faithful and the most important adversary of the death penalty. It is only through the light spread by the socialist parties, it is only by increasing the strength and the culture of the mass of workers, through political and trade union action, that the death penalty—this outrage on civilized humanity—can be effectively fought.

The representatives of the proletariat of every country organized politically and in trade unions, now deliberating at Copenhagen, desire to pillory the active and passive partisans of murder ordered by official civil and military courts. They urge the parliamentary representatives of the working class in every state to demand the abolition of the death penalty on every occasion. Their action in parliament as well as at political events should be made use of, in order to undertake energetic propaganda at public meetings and in the socialist and labor press for the abolition of the death penalty.

* * *

PARTY UNITY

Submitted by the Commission on Resolutions (Fifth Commission), presented to the commission by Paul Louis and later approved by the plenary.

The International Congress calls to mind once more the resolutions of the Amsterdam Congress relating to the unity of the party [see pages 84–85]; and

In consideration that the proletariat is an undivided unity, and consequently every section of the International must form a united and solid group and is bound to get rid of their international divisions in the interest of the working class of their own country and the entire world;

In further consideration that the socialist movement in France is indebted to their unification for an enormous increase of strength and influence:[3]

The Congress urges all national sections that are still divided to unite as soon as possible, and calls on the Bureau to help in bringing this about.

* * *

WAR AND MILITARISM

Resolution of the Commission on Arbitration and Disarmament (Third Commission), adopted unanimously by the congress.

The Congress declares that the armaments of nations have increased alarmingly during recent years in spite of the peace congresses and the protestations of peaceful intentions on the part of the governments. Particularly does this apply to the general movement of the governments to increase naval armaments, whose latest phase is the construction of "dreadnoughts" [battleships]. This policy leads not only to an insane waste of national resources for unproductive purposes—and therefore to the curtailment of means for the realization of necessary social reforms in the interest of the working class—but it also threatens all nations with financial ruin and exhaustion through the unsupportable burdens of indirect taxation.

These armaments have but recently endangered world peace, as they always will. In view of this development, which threatens all the achievements of civilization, the well-being of nations, and the very life of the masses, this Congress reaffirms the resolutions of previous international congresses, and particularly that of the Stuttgart Congress [see pages 103–105].

The workers of all countries have no quarrels or differences that could lead to war. Modern wars are the result of capitalism, and particularly of rivalries of the capitalist classes of the different countries over the world market, and of the spirit of militarism, which is one of the instruments of capitalist class rule and of the economic and political subjugation of the working class. Wars will cease completely only with the disappearance of the capitalist mode of production. The working class, which bears the main burdens of war and suffers most from its effects, has the greatest interest in the prevention of wars. The organized socialist workers of all countries are therefore the only reliable guarantee of universal peace. The Congress therefore again calls upon the labor organizations of all countries to continue a vigorous propaganda of enlightenment among all workers—and particularly among young people—as to the causes of war, in order to educate them in the spirit of international brotherhood.

The Congress, reiterating the oft-repeated duty of socialist representatives in parliament to combat militarism with all means at their command and refusing funds for armaments, requires from its representatives:

(a) To constantly reiterate the demand that international arbitration be made compulsory in all international disputes.

(b) To make persistent and repeated proposals in the direction of ultimate, complete disarmament; and above all, as a first step, the conclusion of a general treaty limiting naval armaments and abrogating the right of seizure at sea.

(c) To demand the abolition of secret diplomacy and the publication of all existing and future agreements between the governments.

(d) To guarantee the self-determination of all nations and their protection from military attacks and forcible subjugation.

The International Socialist Bureau will support all socialist organizations in their fight against militarism by furnishing them with the necessary data and information, and will, when the occasion arrives, endeavor to bring about united action. In case military conflicts arise, this Congress reaffirms the resolution of the Stuttgart Congress, which reads:

> In case of war being imminent, the working class and its parliamentary representatives in the countries concerned shall be bound, with the assistance of the International Socialist Bureau, to do all they can to prevent the outbreak of war, using for this purpose the means that appear to them the most effective, and which must naturally vary according to the acuteness of the class struggle and to the general political conditions.
>
> In case war should break out notwithstanding, they shall be bound to intervene for its speedy termination, and to employ all their forces to utilize the economic and political crisis created by the war in order

to rouse the masses of the people and thereby hasten the downfall of capitalist class rule.

For the proper execution of these measures, the Congress directs the Bureau, in the event of war danger, to take immediate steps to bring about an agreement among the labor parties of the countries affected for united action to prevent the threatened war.

* * *

ON THE HARDIE-VAILLANT AMENDMENT

In the militarism commission, Keir Hardie and Édouard Vaillant had submitted a resolution that read, "Among the means to be used in order to prevent and hinder war, the Congress considers as particularly effective the general strike, especially in the industries that supply war with its implements (arms and ammunition, transport, etc.), as well as propaganda and popular action in their most active forms." This amendment was rejected in the commission by a vote of 131 to 51, with 2 abstentions. But in an effort to avoid a debate on the congress floor on the question of the general strike as a means to prevent war, the following amendment submitted by Émile Vandervelde, Morris Hillquit, F. M. Wibaut, Rosa Luxemburg, Victor Adler, and Friedrich Ebert—and agreed to by Hardie and Vaillant—was approved by the congress.

The Congress decides that the Hardie-Vaillant amendment will be sent to the International Socialist Bureau for study. A report will be submitted to the next International Socialist Congress on the proposals contained in the amendment.

* * *

CARRYING OUT INTERNATIONAL RESOLUTIONS

Resolution of the Commission on Arbitration and Disarmament (Third Commission), and adopted by the congress, with regard to the fight against militarism and war. Originally drafted by Hendrick Van Kol and W. H. Vliegen.

The Congress, recognizing that it would be difficult to come up with written instructions for carrying out the resolutions of international congresses, declares that the power to choose the manner and moment for this must be left up to the national parties.

It nonetheless strongly insists on the duty of parties to do everything possible to carry out the resolutions of international congresses.

The International Bureau will prepare a summary report prior to each international congress on the national parties' implementation of international congress resolutions.

* * *

TRADE UNION UNITY

Resolution of the Commission on Trade Union Questions (Second Commission). Georgy V. Plekhanov reported to the plenary for the commission majority. A minority of the commission, led by Antonín Němec from Czechoslovakia, put forward a resolution calling essentially for absolute autonomy for the union organizations in his country. With his resolution rejected by the commission, Němec presented a minority report to the plenary. The congress adopted the commission majority resolution by a vote of 222 to 5, with 7 abstentions.

The International Socialist Congress in Copenhagen renews the Stuttgart resolution on the relations between the political parties and the trade unions, [see pages 105–107] especially with regard to the point that the unity of the industrial organization should be kept in mind in each state, and is an essential condition of successful struggle against exploitation and oppression.

In multilingual states the united trade unions must, of course, take into account the cultural and linguistic needs of all their members.

The Congress further declares that any attempt to break internationally united trade unions into nationally separate parts contradicts the aim of this resolution of the International Socialist Congress.

The International Socialist Bureau and the International Secretariat of Trade Unions are requested to offer their services to the organizations directly interested, in order to eliminate the conflicts on this subject, in a spirit of socialist good will and brotherhood.

* * *

INTERNATIONAL SOLIDARITY

Resolution of the Commission on Trade Union Questions (Second Commission), originally submitted by the Swedish Social Democratic Party and presented to the congress plenary by August Huggler.

The International Socialist Labor Congress of Copenhagen, emphasizing the essentially international spirit of the proletarian movement and remembering the traditions of active solidarity which owe their origin to the First International, appeals to workers of every country to fulfill their duty of solidarity each time that a struggle between capital and labor takes on such dimensions that it is evident that the workingmen of the country engaged in battle are not able to hold their own against the enemy without help, and that they assist their comrades in the fight by means of subsidies, coming from all sides, according to the proletarian forces of each country.

Such action is all the more necessary since the organization of the opposing forces is being accelerated in proportion as the working class, by its united action, is pressing capitalism. Capitalist power is concentrating itself in gigantic trusts, in cartels, and in national and international employers' unions. On the other hand, the workers are combining their forces, in the first place, in national labor confederations. Under the pressure of this concentration of forces in the two opposed camps, the class struggle alters its aspect and takes new and vaster proportions. One can therefore be prepared for general union struggles, brought about by lockouts on a large scale, such as the one in Denmark of 1899, in Sweden of 1909, or in Germany of 1910.[4] As the class struggle is extended and organized more and more, it will in the future become even more urgently necessary to concentrate the forces of the working class of the whole world, promptly and vigorously, so as to be prepared for the day when workers of every country or of one profession should be threatened with annihilation by the power of the united capitalists.

The Congress requests the International Secretariat of Trade Unions to investigate in what way the international solidarity of the workers may be most expediently organized.

For the near future the Congress recommends:

The more intimate and permanent drawing together of the labor organizations in each country across frontiers.

The revision of the statutes of the societies and federations, with a view to eliminating from these regulations everything that would constitute a hindrance to effective and immediate international action.

The improvement and the extension of international relations of the socialist and labor press. Socialist journalists of a country in which a large conflict is imminent or has already been declared should be particularly requested to transmit prompt and accurate reports of the situation to their foreign colleagues, who, for their part, should utilize them immediately in order everywhere to arouse the sympathetic interest of the working classes, and at the proper time to correct or deny the fantastic and often-too-untrue tales that the press and the agencies in the pay of capital never fail to publish for the purpose of leading public opinion astray.

From this point of view, it is also of the highest importance for the whole labor movement of the world that there should exist everywhere a socialist press that is powerful enough to liberate the masses from the influence and suggestion of the bourgeois press.

* * *

LABOR LEGISLATION

Resolution of the Commission on Labor Legislation and Unemployment (Fourth Commission). Presented to the congress plenary by Hermann Molkenbuhr.

The increasing exploitation of the workers resulting from the development of capitalist production has brought about conditions that render imperative legislation for the protection of the life and health of the worker.

In no country do the laws even approximate that which is absolutely necessary in the interests of the workers, and which could be granted without detriment to existing industry.

The Congress reiterates the following minimum demands regarding legislation for the protection of workers (without distinction of sex) made by the Paris Congress of 1889 [see pags 22–25]:

1. A maximum working day of eight hours.

2. Prohibition of boy and girl labor under fourteen years.

3. Prohibition of night work, except where the nature of the work or the demands of public welfare make it inevitable.

4. Uninterrupted rest of at least thirty-six hours each week for all workers.

5. Complete suppression of the truck system.[5]

6. Absolute right of combination [unionization].

7. Effective and thorough inspection of working conditions, agricultural as well as industrial, with the cooperation of persons elected by the workers.

As a result of the Paris Congress, conferences of governments were held in Berlin in 1890 and in Bern in 1906, and international proposals were made for the protection of workers.[6] But in spite of the lengthy negotiations very little positive legislation has resulted because of the opposition of the governing classes, who fear that their class interests would be injured thereby in spite of the fact that in no country has any branch of industry suffered from the protection of the workers; rather, the improvement of the health and efficiency of the workers has benefited general civilization and also the employing class.

To prevent the workers from falling into pauperism, the Amsterdam Congress demanded adequate measures for the support and care of the sick, those disabled by accident, the old, the invalids, pregnant women and mothers in childbed, widows, orphans, and the unemployed; the administration of such measures to be under the control of the workers, and the same treatment to be given to foreigners [immigrants] as to those belonging to the country [native-born workers]. [See page 87.]

The existing laws for the protection and insurance of the workers are totally inadequate to meet the necessary and justifiable requirements of the workers. Only by the tenacious persistence of the workers can further reforms be obtained.

The Congress therefore calls upon the workers of all nations, whether occupied in industry, in commerce, in agriculture, or in any other branch, to break down the opposition of the governing classes and, by unceasing agitation, and strong and perfect organization, both political and industrial, to win for themselves real and effective protection.

* * *

THE RIGHT OF ASYLUM

Presented by the Commission on Resolutions (Fifth Commission), original-
ly submitted by Wilhelm Ellenbogen, Keir Hardie, Jean Longuet, and I. A.
Rubanovich. The reporter to the congress for the commission was Hardie.

Recently in various countries many instances have occurred where, under various fallacious pretexts, the right of asylum for political refugees has been violated. The Russian government particularly distinguishes itself in this field in a most deplorable manner. Thus Julius Wezosal has been recently arrested in Boston upon the demand of Russia for his extradition.[7]

Even England, contrary to all her traditions, consents to employ this process, violating the right of asylum, as in the case of the revolutionary Hindu, Savarkar, who, in an unprecedented manner, has been arrested on French soil and extradited without any legal formality.[8]

The Congress vigorously protests against these criminal violations of the right of asylum, and urges the proletariat of all countries to resist, by all the means of propaganda and agitation it possesses, these assaults upon the dignity and independence of their own countries, which menace the liberty of action of the working class and its international solidarity.

* * *

ON COOPERATIVES AND COOPERATION

The following resolution was presented to the congress plenary by the Commission on Cooperation (First Commission). Two main lines were debated in the commission: those who saw cooperatives as a weapon in the class struggle, and those who viewed cooperatives primarily as a model of the future socialist society. The resolution adopted largely reflected the first view. One of the participants in the congress commission was V. I. Lenin, who submitted his own resolution to the commission (see the appendix, pages 159–60). The following compromise resolution was adopted by the commission, with two votes against (František Modráček and Lenin). It was presented to the congress plenary by Benno Karpeles, and adopted with a handful of votes against. Although Lenin opposed the resolution in the commission, he voted for it at the plenary.[9]

Taking into consideration that distributive cooperative societies are not only able to secure for their members immediate material advantages, but are also capable of first increasing the influence of the proletariat by the elimination of private commercial enterprise, and, secondly, by bettering the condition of the working classes by means of productive services organized by themselves, and by educating the workers in the independent democratic management of social means of exchange and production:

Considering also that cooperation alone is incapable of realizing the aim of socialism, which is the acquisition of political power for the purpose of collective ownership of the means of production:

This Congress declares, while warning the working classes against the theory maintaining that cooperation by itself is sufficient, that the working class has the strongest interest in utilizing the weapon of cooperation in the class struggle, and urges all socialists and all members of trade unions to take part in the cooperative movement, in order to develop themselves in the spirit of socialism and keep the cooperative societies from any deviation from the path of education and the promotion of working-class solidarity.

The socialist members of cooperative societies are urged to endeavor in these societies to see that the profits are not entirely returned to the members, but that part is devoted either by the society itself or by the federation of wholesale societies, to the development of production and to education and instruction, in order:

1. That the conditions of wages and work in the cooperative societies shall be regulated in accordance with trade union rules.

2. That the organization of the conditions of employment in cooperative societies shall be the best possible, and that no purchases of goods shall be made without regard to the condition of the producer.

It is left to the cooperative organizations of each country to decide for themselves whether and to what extent they will aid from their resources the political and trade union movement.

Furthermore, being convinced that the services that cooperation can render to the working class will be the greater in proportion as the cooperative movement is itself strong and united, the Congress declares that it is desirable that the cooperative societies of each country constituted on this basis and subscribing to this present resolution should form a single federation.

It declares, besides, that the working class in its struggle against capitalism is especially concerned that trade unions, cooperative societies, and the Socialist Party, while preserving each its own unity and autonomy, should enter into closer and closer relations with one another.

* * *

ON JAPAN

Submitted by the Commission on Resolutions (Fifth Commission).

The International Socialist Congress of Copenhagen emphatically condemns the measures taken by the Japanese government to oppress the socialist labor movement in that country—measures showing that the true character of this government is a mixture of arbitrary absolutism and of capitalist brutality. These measures have as their aim to make impossible any effort of the Japanese proletariat toward liberty, emancipation, and culture, and to bring them down to the level of an impotent and helpless class.[10]

This Congress, recognizing the immense importance of the emancipation of the Japanese proletariat for the liberation of the proletariat of the entire world, is conscious that the development of capitalism now going on in Asia in so rapid a manner prepares the soil for the socialist seed; it assures the young proletariat of Japan, which is awakening and which desires to struggle against its cruel exploiters, of the fullest sympathy of all the socialist parties.

The Congress is only doing its duty in expressing from its heart its recognition of and admiration for the valiant and intrepid fighters in the vanguard of socialism in Japan, who alone and under the most difficult conditions lead the battle against the external policy of warlike expansion and the international policy of oppression, and who, by that, serve the cause of the international proletariat in a very real manner.

* * *

ON ARGENTINA

Submitted by the Commission on Resolutions (Fifth Commission).

The International Congress condemns the attitude of the oligarchy, which systematically falsifies universal suffrage, which tramples underfoot as well the united political action of the working class.[11] This oligarchy incites violent acts and puts itself in the service of native and foreign capital, keeping the people in a state of the deepest degradation and offering them a demoralizing spectacle of anarchy.

The International Socialist Congress condemns these disgraceful conditions in Argentina in the sharpest manner possible. It welcomes the attitude of the Argentinian Socialist Party in the difficult circumstances in which they are placed, and hopes that their endeavors will succeed in enlightening the workers of Argentina and awakening them to class consciousness, securing with that the political and economic progress of the country.

* * *

THE SITUATION IN TURKEY

Submitted by the Commission on Resolutions (Fifth Commission).

In consideration of:

1. The colonial policy practiced by the European capitalist states in regard to Turkey;

2. The proclamation of a constitution, which confers on each citizen the rights of man and of citizen;

3. The violation of the rights of union and to strike by the government of Turkey;

4. The disastrous consequences of an autocratic policy in regard to the laboring class of Turkey;

The International Socialist Congress of Copenhagen declares:

That the abominable capitalist and colonial policy of the European states can be effectively combated only by democratic and constitutional reforms in the Balkan states and by a peaceful understanding among the sovereign peoples of these states, such as today is alone represented by Social Democracy in opposition to the governments of the Balkans as of other European states.

The Congress protests against the reactionary policy of the Young Turk government, and especially against the laws directed against the trade unions and strikes, and sends its fraternal greetings to the emerging socialist movement in Turkey.[12]

***

ON SPAIN

Submitted by the Commission on Resolutions (Fifth Commission). Presented to the congress plenary by Rosa Luxemburg and Jean Longuet.

The International Socialist Congress of Copenhagen, in view of the tragic events of which Spain—and in particular Catalonia—has been the theater during the past year, expresses its complete sympathy with the comrades of the Spanish Socialist Party, the militants of Catalonia, and all the organized workers of Spain who, in accordance with the decisions of the International, by the collective action of the proletariat, opposed the colonial adventure in Morocco, [13] protests against the barbarous repression of which our comrades of Barcelona and other towns have been the victims and, in particular, against the pseudo-juridical assassination of Ferrer, and welcomes the election of Comrade Iglesias, the first representative of the working class elected in the capital of the monarchy itself,[14] as a decisive sign of the awakening class consciousness of the Spanish workers.

***

ON PERSIA

Submitted by the Commission on Resolutions (Fifth Commission).

Considering:

That since the commencement of the Persian [Iranian] revolution and in consequence of the Anglo-Russian agreement, the tsar's government has used every means possible to bring about the failure of the constitutional movement;

That on several occasions they even intervened with an armed force under the pretext of maintaining order on their frontiers and protecting the lives of their own subjects in Persia, but in reality with the obvious aim of impeding the efforts of the Persian democrats, that these troops and the Russian police in the province of Azerbaijan (Tabriz)[15] openly dealt rigorously with the insurgents and the leaders belonging to the Dashnaktsutyun party;[16]

That the Russian government even now, through the intermediary of its many secret agents, continues its intrigues and provocations in Persia;

That a considerable number of troops still remain on Persian territory, in spite of the reiterated protests of the Majlis and of the cabinet at Tehran;

That the same Russian government is actively "at work" in Turkey, especially in Armenian Turkey, for the purpose of stirring up the feudal Kurds, the most reactionary element of Turkey,[17] against the Armenians, thus fomenting disturbances and provoking a counterrevolution;

That the Russian ambassadors at Constantinople and Tcharikooff [Charykov] and the Russian consul at Erzerum have had special instructions to this effect;[18]

Considering, in short:

That tsarism, victorious in its march to kill liberty in its own territories and profoundly hating the constitutional order established on its two frontiers, is attempting, systematically and with perseverance, to restore the regime of absolutism in Persia and Turkey.

In the presence of these two grave facts, which constitute a permanent danger for the two young democracies of the East:

The Congress calls upon the socialist parties of Europe to use all the means in their power to put an end to the reactionary dealing of tsarism.

* * *

ON FINLAND

Submitted by the Commission on Resolutions (Fifth Commission). The resolution was drafted by socialists from Russia and Finland, and was presented to the commission by Charles Rappoport of France.

The International Socialist Congress in Copenhagen strongly condemns the barbarous and dishonest policy of the Russian government and the reactionary representatives of the possessing class in the Duma and the Council of State—a policy that aims at the total suppression of the autonomy and of the liberty won by Finland, and a policy that will make it the most oppressed province in the empire.

The Congress affirms that by its policy toward Finland, the tsarist government has cynically taken back all the guarantees solemnly given in 1905 and has suppressed its secular constitution in defiance of the formal will of the Finnish people, of the best part of European opinion, and of the opinion of the most eminent jurists.[19]

It also affirms that the brutal suppression of Finnish autonomy is only one consequence of a whole system of savage oppression of all nationalities, non-Russian equally with Russian, an oppression carried out by a band of assassins cloaking themselves with a pretended constitutionalism.

Seeing that the ruling classes of Europe and the great organs of the press, while they formulate platonic professions in favor of Finland, in fact sustain tyranny by all the means at their disposal, and seeing that the Finnish socialists are engaged in a serious struggle to save democratic liberty and the right of the Finnish people to control themselves, which concerns not only socialism but democratic liberty, the Congress expresses its confidence in the energy, the courage, and the perseverance of the proletariat of Finland.

It is convinced that the proletariat of Finland will march on in accord with the working class of Russia, struggling in solidarity against the same regime of oppression.

It urges all the socialist parties and all the sincere democrats of the entire world to protest, by every means in their power (press, parliament, public meetings, etc.), against the *coup de force* directed against Finland. The Congress instructs the International Socialist Bureau to take steps to organize in every country a demonstration as complete and powerful as possible of the socialist proletariat in favor of Finland.

* * *

ON MOROCCO

Resolution drafted by French and Spanish delegates and presented to the congress plenary by Pablo Iglesias. It was adopted unanimously.

The socialist delegates from France and Spain to the Copenhagen Congress propose by common agreement the following resolution:
The Congress,

Recalling the decision taken by the Stuttgart Congress with regard to the French-Spanish undertakings in Morocco [see page 114];

Considering that the French socialists have once again protested the incursions by certain generals into Moroccan territory;

That on the Spanish side, military preparations are hastily being made for a new campaign.

That the daily threats constitute a burden on the two nations and on southern Europe as a whole, as a result of capitalist appetites:

Urges the socialist parties of all countries—and especially the workers of France and Spain—to assist more than ever the mobilization of the socialist parties of these two nations, an initiative glorified by the heroism of revolutionaries in Barcelona and other centers, and to do everything in their power to oppose all new military expeditions.

9.

Basel Congress, November 24–25, 1912

In October 1912, Montenegro, Bulgaria, Serbia, and Greece declared war on the Ottoman Empire, launching the First Balkan War. Many feared that this conflict could become the spark that would ignite a European-wide conflagration.

With that danger in mind, the International Socialist Bureau encouraged antiwar meetings throughout Europe and organized an Extraordinary International Socialist Congress, held in Basel, Switzerland. The congress was attended by 545 delegates from twenty-two countries.

The Basel Congress issued a manifesto, largely based on the Stuttgart resolution on war and militarism, but also going farther in its depiction of the imperialist nature of the war drive.

Among those who recognized the Basel Manifesto's importance was Lenin. In the years after 1914, he repeatedly pointed to the revolutionary nature of this document, defending it against the practices of the majority of the Second International, which had gone over to support the war effort of their respective capitalist classes. "The [Basel] Manifesto is but the fruit of the great propaganda work carried on throughout the entire epoch of the Second International," Lenin stated.[1]

THE BASEL MANIFESTO ON WAR AND MILITARISM

The International, at its congresses at Stuttgart and Copenhagen, laid down the following principle for the war against war:

> In case of war being imminent, the working class and its parliamentary representatives in the countries concerned shall be bound, with the assistance of the International Socialist Bureau, to do all they can to prevent the outbreak of war, using for this purpose the means that appear to them the most effective, and which must naturally vary according to the acuteness of the class struggle and to the general political conditions.
>
> In case war should break out notwithstanding, they shall be bound to intervene for its speedy termination, and to employ all their forces to utilize the economic and political crisis created by the war in order to rouse the masses of the people and thereby hasten the downfall of capitalist class rule.

Recent events have more than ever made it the duty of the proletariat to use all their energy to carry out organized action. On the one hand, the general mad rivalry in armaments, by increasing the cost of living, has intensified class antagonisms and created an implacable spirit of revolt in the working class. The workers want to stop this system of extravagant waste and consequent unrest. On the other hand, the periodically recurring threats of war are getting more and more critical. The great nations of Europe are constantly on the verge of being driven against each other, without the slightest pretext of real national interests for such attacks on reason and humanity.

The Balkan crisis, which is already responsible for such terrible horrors, would mean the most fearful danger for civilization and the workers if allowed to spread.[2] It would be at the same time one of the greatest outrages of history through the discrepancy between the immensity of the catastrophe and the insignificance of the interests involved.

For this reason the Congress rejoices at the complete unanimity of socialist parties and labor unions in all countries in the war against war. The workers of all countries have risen at the same time against imperialism; each section of the International is offering proletarian resistance to the government of its country and mobilizing public opinion of their nation against all warlike ideas, thus laying the foundation for strong cooperation of the workers of all lands, which has already contributed to saving the threatened peace of the world. The ruling classes' fear that a revolution by the proletariat will follow a world war has been an essential guarantee of peace.

The Congress therefore asks socialist parties to continue their work by all possible means at their command. Each socialist party will contribute its own action to this common end.

The socialist parties in the Balkan Peninsula have a difficult task. The great powers of Europe, by a systematic neglect of all reform in Turkey, have contributed to creating economic and political disorder, stirring up national passions, leading to revolt and war. As against exploiting these conditions in the interests of the dynasties and the capitalists, the socialist parties of the Balkans, with admirable courage, put forward the demand for a democratic federation.

The Congress urges them to continue this commendable line of action, and believes that the Social Democracy of the Balkans will do everything to prevent the results of the war, bought with such terrible sacrifices, from being exploited by the dynasties, the militarists, and the capitalist classes of the Balkan states for their own selfish and expansionist interests. Above all, the Congress urges the Balkan socialists to oppose everything likely to lead to a renewal of the old animosities between Serbians, Bulgarians, Romanians, and Greeks, as well as to all violence against Balkan peoples whom they now combat as enemies: the Turks and the Albanians. The socialists of the Balkans must strongly oppose oppression of these peoples, combat inflamed national chauvinism, and proclaim the fraternity of all Balkan peoples, including Turks, Albanians, and Romanians.

The socialist parties of Austria-Hungary, Croatia, Slavonia, Bosnia, and Herzegovina must continue with all their strength their hitherto successful efforts to prevent any attack by the Austrian monarchy upon Serbia. They must continue to oppose in the future, as they have done up to the present, any attempt to violently seize from Serbia the fruits of the war, to transform that country into an Austrian province, and to embroil the peoples of Austria-Hungary and the other nations of Europe in conflict in the interests of the ruling dynasty. The socialists of Austria-Hungary will have to struggle in the future to secure a completely autonomous and democratic government for the whole of the southern Slavic nations now governed by the Habsburg dynasty within the frontiers of Austria-Hungary.

The socialists of Austria-Hungary and also of Italy have to pay special attention to the Albanian question. The Congress recognizes the right to autonomy of the Albanian nation, but protests against the fact that under the mask of autonomy Albania might fall into the hands of Austro-Hungarian and Italian usurpation, which would not only be a danger for Albania, but might over time threaten the peace between Austria and Italy. Albania can live in real independence only as an autonomous member of a democratic Balkan Federation. Therefore, the Congress urges the socialists of Austria-Hungary and Italy to protest against all actions by their governments to draw Albania into their spheres of influence. Socialists must continue their efforts to consolidate peaceful relations between Austria-Hungary and Italy.

The Congress heartily salutes the protest strikes of the Russian workers, thus proving that the Russian and Polish working class is beginning to recover from the blows received during the tsar's counterrevolution. The Congress sees therein a guarantee against the criminal intrigues of tsarism, which, after having shed the blood of the Russian people and after having so often betrayed and delivered the Balkan nations to their enemies, is staggering between the fear of the consequences that a war would have for them, and the fear of a nationalist movement it itself created. And if the tsar is once more pretending to play the part of liberator, it is in order to reconquer through this lying trick Russian predominance in the Balkans.

The Congress expects that the strengthened working class of Russia, Poland, and Finland, both in town and country, will tear asunder this mask of lies, oppose all bellicose adventures, and resist every tsarist attack, whether upon Armenia or Constantinople, by devoting their every energy towards renewing their revolutionary opposition to tsarism. If tsarism is the hope of all reactionary forces of Europe, it is also the bitterest foe of democracy and of the peoples over whom it rules. It is therefore the bounden duty of the International to bring about its downfall.

The most important task of the International falls on the working class of Germany, France, and Great Britain, to demand from their governments to withhold all support to either Austria or Russia, to abstain from all intervention in the Balkan troubles, and in every respect to observe strict neutrality. A war between the three great nations over an outlet to the sea, concerning which Austria and Serbia are in dispute, would be criminal madness. The workers of Germany and France do not recognize that any secret treaties necessitate any obligation to intervene in the Balkan conflict.

If, however, as a consequence of the military defeat of Turkey, the downfall of the Ottoman power in Asia Minor becomes inevitable, it would be the duty of British, French, and German socialists to oppose with all their might the policy of conquest of Asia Minor, since the result would inevitably be a world war.

The Congress is of the opinion that the greatest danger to European peace is the artificially maintained animosity between Great Britain and Germany. The Congress therefore salutes the working class of the two countries for their efforts to improve the situation. It believes that the best means of removing friction would be an understanding between Germany and Great Britain to halt the increase of their respective fleets and to suppress the seizure of private property at sea. The Congress urges the socialists of Great Britain and Germany to continue their agitation for such an agreement. To overcome all outstanding differences between Germany, on the one side, and Great Britain, on the other, would be to remove the greatest danger to world peace. It would weaken the mighty position of tsarism, now trying to strengthen itself owing to these differences. It would make impossible an attack on Serbia by Austria, and would finally secure peace to the world. To this end, above all, the efforts of the international movement must be directed.

The Congress declares the foregoing to be the policy of the Socialist International and expects all affiliated organizations to agree to uphold these principles of foreign policy. It urges the workers of all countries to oppose the power of capitalist imperialism through international working-class solidarity. It wants the ruling classes in all countries to put an end to the economic misery produced by the capitalist system, not to increase it by warlike action. It insists on the demand for peace. Governments must not forget that in the present condition of Europe and the present state of mind of the workers, war will not be without disaster to themselves. They must remember that the Franco-German war resulted in the revolutionary movement of the Commune,[3] that the Russo-Japanese war put into motion the revolutionary movement in Russia, and that the arms race increased class conflicts in England and provoked enormous strikes on the continent.

It would be madness if the governments did not comprehend that the mere notion of a world war will call forth indignation and passion among the workers. Proletarians consider it a crime to shoot each other down in the interests of and for the profit of the capitalists, for the sake of dynastic honor and secret diplomatic treaties.

If the governments cut off even the possibility of normal development of the people and thereby provoke desperate steps, they will have to bear the entire responsibility for the crisis they bring about.

The International will redouble its efforts to avert such a crisis and will spread its views more energetically. The Congress requests the International Socialist Bureau to follow events with redoubled attention, and whatever happens, to keep up communications and relations among the proletarian parties of every country.

The proletariat is aware that at the present moment it is the bearer of the future welfare of humanity. The proletariat will exert all its efforts to prevent the destruction of the youth of the nations menaced by all the horrors of wholesale slaughter, famine, and pestilence.

The Congress appeals to you, proletarians and socialists of all countries, so that in this decisive hour you make your voices heard.

Make known your wishes in every form and everywhere with all your energy. Raise unanimous protests in every parliament, in demonstrations and mass action. Utilize every means that the organization and power of the proletariat place in your hands, in such a way that the governments will constantly feel before them the attentive and active will of the working class for peace.

Against the capitalist world of exploitation and mass murder stands the proletarian world of peace and union among the peoples.

1914—The Collapse of the Second International

Based on the resolutions on war and militarism adopted repeatedly at congresses of the Second International, most class-conscious socialists and unionists were undoubtedly confident that their parties and unions would resist war moves by their governments with energetic, effective, and internationally coordinated action. But less than two years after the Basel Manifesto, that confidence would be shattered.

Following the assassination of Austria-Hungary's Archduke Franz Ferdinand on June 28, 1914, events moved inexorably toward the war that most European powers had long desired and planned for. War declarations began on July 28; within a week most major countries on the continent were swept up into the conflict.

During these weeks, most rank-and-file socialists realized that some kind of a war was imminent. Socialist parties organized large antiwar demonstrations across Europe, and party newspapers denounced militarism and secret diplomacy. Most party leaders, however, believed that their respective capitalist governments genuinely wanted peace and expected them to act to prevent a generalized conflict. The demonstrations therefore rarely took aim at the war preparations of their own rulers.

The International Socialist Bureau held an emergency session in Paris on July 29–30, attended by most major figures in the world socialist movement. But other than giving encouragement to antiwar demonstrations and holding a public meeting in the French capital to advocate peace, little more was done.

Lacking any confidence that the drive toward war could be halted, the dominant mood among the Second International's leaders was resignation. That mood quickly turned first into reluctant acceptance, and finally into outright support for the war effort of their governments.

On August 4 the Social Democratic Party of Germany—the strongest party in the Second International, long considered the bastion of orthodox Marxism—voted unanimously for war credits (military funding) in the German Reichstag. That move was quickly repeated by Social Democratic workers' parties in the other warring countries, apart from those in Russia and Serbia. Symbolizing this capitulation to national chauvinism, the Second International's president, Émile Vandervelde, joined the Belgian government as minister of state.

These steps were all in direct violation of multiple resolutions adopted at Second International congresses. As such, the events of 1914 marked the death of the Second International as a revolutionary movement. Henceforth the leaderships of most Social Democratic parties tied their fate to the success of the capitalist rulers in their own countries. Thousands of Social Democrats in all countries were drafted into the army, where they were encouraged by their party leaderships to devote themselves to killing their party comrades and other workers on the opposite side of the trenches.

Reflecting this collapse, the very concept of internationalism began to be questioned by many socialists. A November 1914 article by Karl Kautsky reflected a mood of demoralization: "We deluded ourselves in expecting that the International would be able to bring about a united stance of the whole world Socialist proletariat during a world war. . . . The World War has divided socialists into different camps, for the most part into different national camps. The International cannot prevent that. In other words the International is not an effective tool in wartime."[1]

Left-wing, antiwar, and revolutionary socialists rejected this stance of resignation, however. Through witnessing all these bitter developments, a small but growing number of socialists concluded that the opportunist trend that had long been building within the Second International had finally reached its culmination point. One such individual was Lenin, who began to raise the need to create a new International.

An initial step in reestablishing international relations was taken by Clara Zetkin, as secretary of the International Socialist Women's Bureau, who convened a Conference of Socialist Women in Bern,

Switzerland, March 26–28, 1915. This gathering was followed a week later by an International Socialist Youth Conference in the same city.

Out of these initiatives, a conference of revolutionary and anti-war socialists took place in Zimmerwald, Switzerland, in September 1915, launching what became known as the Zimmerwald movement. Subsequent conferences of this movement were held in Kienthal, Switzerland, in April 1916, and in Stockholm, Sweden, in September 1917.

One month after the Stockholm conference, the October Revolution in Russia erupted. Over the next three years, socialist parties split in two between those who identified with the Bolsheviks and supported the road Russian revolutionaries had embarked on, and those who rejected this road. Some tried for a time to straddle the two poles, but all ultimately came down on one side or the other.

Two rival international congresses were held in early 1919, codifying the split on a world level.

A congress in Bern, Switzerland, in early February 1919, officially reconstituted the Second International. But the new body bore little resemblance to the one that Frederick Engels helped form in 1889. Instead of a revolutionary opponent of capitalism, it had now become in practice a defender of that system, with a few reforms. At the Bern Congress, a bland assessment of the 1914 collapse was offered in the opening address by Karl Hjalmar Branting of Sweden, who was careful to avoid any blame:

> Already since the Stuttgart Congress of 1907 the struggle against war and militarism has been our foremost concern. We all perceived, through our common intuition, the forces which must endanger the peace of the world in a society which not only gave free scope to the capitalistic policy of exploitation, but which, besides, maintained in the greater parts of the world a concentration of power in the hands of feudal castes, which was altogether out of touch with the real thought of the peoples and divested of responsibility. The International could still raise its voice at Basle in 1912 against the already threatening universal war. In 1914, however, when the contest had already become more openly acute and when, moreover, criminal hopes for a war which should speedily bring the domination of the world within the grasp of one strong nation, set at naught all attempts towards

a peaceful compromise on the part of the western democracies, the International itself fell a first victim to the world-catastrophe.[2]

No discussion on the reasons for this catastrophic collapse occurred at the Bern Congress.

A competing congress was held the following month in Moscow, on March 2–6, 1919, founding a Third International—the Communist International. The balance sheet drawn by this gathering on the efforts to create an international revolutionary working-class movement was sharply different:

> Conscious of the world-historic character of their tasks, advanced workers have striven for an international association since their first steps to organize the socialist movement. The cornerstone was laid in 1864 in London with the founding of the First International. The Franco-Prussian War, out of which Hohenzollern Germany emerged, cut the ground from under the First International while at the same time giving impetus to the development of national workers' parties. Already in 1889, these parties came together at the Paris congress and created the organization of the Second International. But in that period, the center of gravity of the workers' movement remained entirely on national soil, within the framework of the national state, based on national industry, and working within national parliamentarism. Decades of organizational and reform work created a generation of leaders who in their majority verbally acknowledged the program of social revolution, but renounced it in reality and became mired in reformism and in adaptation to the bourgeois state.
>
> The opportunist character of the Second International's leading parties was completely exposed and caused the greatest debacle in world history at the moment when the course of events called for revolutionary methods of struggle by the workers' parties. If the war of 1870 dealt a blow to the First International by revealing that the power of united masses did not stand behind its revolutionary socialist program, so too the war of 1914 killed the Second International by revealing that above the solidly welded masses stood parties that had become servile organs of the bourgeois state.[3]

These two contrasting assessments highlight the fact that despite its ignominious collapse, the Second International of 1889–1914 nevertheless remained an essential part of the continuity of all major currents in the workers' movement, as well as a point of reference that had to be addressed in one way or another. They also go to the heart of the ongoing battle over the Second International's legacy.

* * *

Reviving and popularizing the concept of international working-class unity in action was perhaps the primary accomplishment of the Second International during the quarter century when its resolutions were guided by revolutionary Marxism. By winning broad masses to socialism, it helped provide a seedbed for revolutionary movements that began to germinate during the great working-class upsurge that followed the end of World War I—even though many of these movements developed in polar opposition to what most parties of the Second International had become by that point.

The founding congress of the Second International in 1889 took an important step in promoting international solidarity with the establishment of May Day as an occasion for international working-class action. The very next year, Frederick Engels took part in a May 1890 demonstration in London of two hundred thousand working people, which was part of the internationally coordinated actions. Giving his assessment of this historic manifestation of proletarian unity, Engels wrote what can be considered an accurate summation of the Second International's accomplishments and the most positive aspects of its legacy:

> "Working men of all countries, unite!" But few voices responded when we proclaimed these words to the world forty-two years ago, on the eve of the first Paris revolution [of 1848] in which the proletariat came out with demands of its own. On September 28, 1864, however, the proletarians of most of the Western European countries joined hands in the International Working Men's Association of glorious memory. True, the International itself lived only nine years. But that the eternal union of the proletarians of all countries created by it is still alive and lives stronger than ever, there is no better witness than this day. Because today, as I write these lines, the European and American proletariat is reviewing its fighting forces, mobilised for the first time, mobilised as *one* army, under *one* flag, for *one* immediate aim: the standard eight-hour working day to be established by legal enactment, as proclaimed by the Geneva Congress of the International in 1866 and again by the Paris Workers' Congress in 1889. And today's spectacle will open the eyes of the capitalists and

landlords of all countries to the fact that today the working men of all countries are united indeed.

If only Marx were still by my side to see this with his own eyes![4]

APPENDIXES

DUTCH RESOLUTION ON GENERAL
STRIKE AGAINST WAR (1891)

Counterresolution presented by Ferdinand Domela Nieuwenhuis, for the Dutch delegation, to the resolution on militarism adopted by the Brussels Congress (see pages 35–36).

The Congress:

Considering that national divergences are never in the interests of proletarians, but rather of their oppressors;

Considering that all modern wars, provoked exclusively by the capitalist class, are intended in the hands of that class to break the power of the revolutionary movement and to consolidate the supremacy of the bourgeoisie through the continuation of the most shameful exploitation;

Considering that at present European governments cannot invoke the excuse of having been provoked to war, on account of war being the result of the international will of capitalism:

The Socialist International Congress of Brussels decides that socialists of all countries will oppose to the proclamation of war an appeal for the people to strike.

* * *

FRENCH GENERAL STRIKE RESOLUTION (1896)

Below is the minority report and motion from the Economic and Industrial Commission of the London Congress, put forward by Eugène Guérard of the

French rail workers' union. It was rejected by a large majority of the congress. For the commission report that was approved, see pages 56–61.

Seeing that at several French national congresses—Marseilles (1892), Paris (1893), Nantes (1894), and Limoges (1895)—the trade unionists have declared in favor of a general strike in all trades as a method of emancipation;

That in Belgium a general strike, even though imperfectly organized, had a great effect in obtaining the suffrage from the bourgeoisie.[1]

That Sweden and Austria in their fight to obtain this same right have adopted the same means;

That if *a priori* the general international strike seems to be impossible, it may be very different with a general national strike;

But that, as a matter of fact, the question of a national strike has not been sufficiently investigated in the different countries;

Therefore the Congress invites the workers of all nations, and in particular the trade unionists, to study this important question, which may be decided at the next congress.

* * *

GUESDE-FERRI RESOLUTION (1900)

The text below was put forward at the Paris Congress by Jules Guesde and Enrico Ferri in opposition to the Kautsky resolution on "Socialists in Public Office and Alliances with Bourgeois Parties" (see pages 77–78). In the congress plenary, the Guesde-Ferri resolution was defeated by a vote of 29 to 9. But its conclusions were largely incorporated in the Dresden-Amsterdam resolution approved by the 1904 congress.

The Fifth International Congress, meeting in Paris, declares again that the conquest of public power refers to the political expropriation of the capitalist class, whether this expropriation takes place peacefully or violently.

As a result, under the capitalist system, it allows only for the occupation of elected positions that the [Socialist] Party can capture by means of its own forces, that is, workers organized in a class party. It thereby prohibits any socialist participation in bourgeois governments, against which socialists must remain in irreconcilable opposition.

* * *

ADLER-VANDERVELDE RESOLUTION (1904)

The following was put forward at the Amsterdam Congress by Victor Adler and Émile Vandervelde as a counterresolution to the Dresden-Amsterdam resolution on tactics (see pages 83–84). The main thrust of the resolution was to endorse the "exceptional cases" clause of the 1900 Kautsky resolution that left open the possibility of socialist participation in capitalist governments. In the commission taking up the question, the Vandervelde-Adler resolution was rejected by a vote of 24 to 16. Following the debate in the congress plenary, it failed to obtain a majority in a tie vote of 21 to 21.

The Congress affirms in the most strenuous way the necessity of maintaining unwaveringly our tried and glorious tactics based on the class war and shall never allow that the conquest of the political power in the teeth of the bourgeoisie shall be replaced by a policy of concession to the established order.

The result of this policy of concession would be to change a party that pursues the swiftest possible transformation of bourgeois society into a socialist society—consequently revolutionary in the best sense of the word—into a party that contents itself with reforming bourgeois society.

For this reason, the Congress, persuaded that class antagonisms, far from diminishing, increase continually, states:

1. That the party declines all responsibility whatsoever for the political and economic conditions based on capitalist production and consequently cannot approve of any means that tend to maintain in power the dominant class;

2. That the Social Democracy, in regard to the dangers and the inconveniences of the participation in the government in bourgeois society, brings to mind and confirms the Kautsky resolution, passed at the International Congress of Paris in 1900.

* * *

IMMIGRATION COMMISSION RESOLUTIONS (1904)

The following two counterposed resolutions from the Amsterdam Congress Commission on Emigration and Immigration were laid before the congress plenary. The majority resolution was presented to the congress by Manuel Ugarte of Argentina. The minority resolution was submitted by Hendrick Van Kol, Morris Hillquit, Claude Thompson, Hermann Schlüter, Algernon Lee, and P. Verdorst. After some discussion, a motion by Keir Hardie was adopted to not vote on the resolutions due to shortness of time, and to hold the question over until the next congress. The Stuttgart Congress of 1907 essentially approved the perspective of the majority resolution.

MAJORITY RESOLUTION

The Congress declares that immigrant workers are the victims of the capitalist system, which often forces them to emigrate so as to painfully secure their existence and liberty.

Immigrant workers are often used to replace workers on strike, resulting occasionally in bloody conflicts between workers of different nationalities.

The Congress condemns all legislation designed to prevent emigration.

It declares that propaganda to enlighten emigrants attracted artificially by capitalist entrepreneurs, through often-false information, is absolutely essential.

It is convinced that, owing to socialist propaganda and workers' organization, immigrants will, after a time, be won to the side of the organized workers of the countries of emigration and will demand legal wages.

The Congress further declares that it is useful for socialist representatives in parliament to demand that through tight and effective measures, governments seek to control the numerous abuses that immigration gives rise to. Socialists in parliament should also propose legislative reforms so that migrant workers acquire political and civil rights in countries of emigration as rapidly as possible, with their rights restored as soon as they return to their countries of origin, or that the various countries ensure immigrants the same rights through reciprocity agreements.

The Congress urges socialist parties and trade union federations to work more vigorously than they have done thus far to spread propaganda among the immigrant workers concerning the organization of workers and international solidarity.

MINORITY RESOLUTION

Fully considering the dangers connected with the immigration of foreign workingmen, inasmuch as it brings on a reduction of wages and furnishes the material for strikebreakers, occasionally also for bloody conflicts between workingmen, the Congress declares:

That under the influence and agitation from socialist and trade union quarters, the immigrants will gradually rank themselves on the side of the native workers and demand the same wages that the latter demand.

Therefore, the Congress condemns all legislative enactment that forbids or hinders the immigration of foreign workingmen whom misery forces to emigrate.

In further consideration of the fact that workers of backward races (Chinese, Negroes, etc.) are often imported by capitalists in order to keep down the native workers by means of cheap labor, and that this cheap labor, which constitutes a willing object of exploitation, lives in an ill-concealed state of slavery, the Congress declares that the Social Democracy is bound to combat with all its energy the application of this means, which serves to destroy the organization of labor, and thereby to hamper the progress and the eventual realization of socialism.

* * *

DUTCH COLONIAL RESOLUTION (1904)

This resolution, submitted by the Dutch party for discussion at the Amsterdam Congress and presumably drafted by Hendrick Van Kol, was circulated to all parties prior to the congress. It presents the "socialist colonialism" perspective that Van Kol had begun to promote. However, no discussion of this resolution appears in the official record of the deliberations of the Amsterdam Congress's commission on the colonial question nor in the plenary itself.

The International Socialist Congress at Amsterdam declares that Social Democrats are obliged to define their position regarding colonial policy for the following reasons:

1. Historical development has given to several countries colonies, economically bound by close ties to their mother country, politically unaccustomed to self-government, so that it would be impossible to leave them to themselves, if only from the point of view of international relations.

2. Modern capitalism is pushing civilized countries on to continuous expansion, both to open new outlets for their products and to find fields for the easy increase of their capital. This policy of conquest—often joined with crimes and pillage, having no other aim than to quench the capitalists' insatiable thirst for gold, and forcing ever greater expenditures for the increase of militarism—must be opposed implacably. It is this that leads nations along the road of protectionism and of chauvinism, constituting a perpetual menace of international conflicts, and above all, aggravating the crushing burden on the proletariat, and retarding its emancipation.

3. The new wants that will make themselves felt after the victory of the working class and from the time of its economic emancipation, will make necessary, even under the socialist system of the future, the possession of colonies. Modern countries can no longer dispense with countries furnishing certain raw materials and tropical products indispensable to the industry and the needs of humanity, until such time as these can be produced by the exchange of the products of home industry and commerce.

The Social Democratic Party, which has economic development and the class struggle as the foundations of its political action, and which, in conformity with its principles, its aims, and its tendencies, severely condemns all exploitation and oppression of individuals, classes, and nations, accepts the following rules to define its colonial policy:

Capitalism being an inevitable stage of economic evolution that the colonies also must traverse, it will be necessary to make room for the development of industrial capitalism, even by sacrificing, if necessary, the old forms of property (communal or feudal).

But at the same time, the Social Democracy should struggle with all its strength against the degenerating influence of this capitalist development upon the colonial proletariat, and so much the more because it may be foreseen that the latter will not be capable of struggling for itself.

With a view to improving the condition of the laborers, as well as to prevent all the profits being taken away from the colonies, thus impoverishing them, the operation by the state of suitable industries will be useful or necessary, in conjunction with the operation of others by private parties. This will serve alike to hasten the process of capitalist development and to improve the social status of the native laborer.

It will then be the duty of the Social Democracy to favor the organization of the modern proletariat in all countries where it shall arise, to increase its strength of resistance in its struggle against capitalism, and, by raising its wages, to avert for the old capitalist countries the dangers of the murderous competition of the cheap labor of these primitive peoples.

To lift up the natives with a view to democratic self-government should be the supreme aim of our colonial policy, the details of which will be elaborated in a national program for each particular colonial group.

In view of these considerations, the Amsterdam Congress holds that it is the duty of the socialist parties of all countries:

1. To oppose by all means in their power the policy of capitalist conquest.

2. To formulate in a program the rules to be followed in their colonial policy, based on the principles enunciated in this resolution.

**

COLONIAL COMMISSION MAJORITY RESOLUTION (1907)

Resolution of the Colonial Commission majority, which was rejected by the Stuttgart Congress. For the resolution adopted by the congress, see pages 107–108.

The Congress while pointing out that in general the usefulness or necessity of colonies, especially in the working class, is greatly exaggerated, does not condemn in principle and for all time every colonial policy which under a socialist regime may become a work of civilization.

In reaffirmation of the Paris (1900) and Amsterdam (1904) resolutions. . . . [*The next four paragraphs are the same as the ones finally approved.*]

To this effect the socialist members of parliament must propose to their governments to create an international understanding, with a view to establish an international agreement for the protection of the right of the aborigines, the execution of which shall be mutually guaranteed by the contracting countries.

**

AMERICAN SP RESOLUTION ON IMMIGRATION (1907)

The following resolution of the American Socialist Party, which had been submitted to the Stuttgart Congress, was defended at Stuttgart by Morris Hillquit. The decisive part of the resolution is point 3, with its implied support for immigration restrictions. For the text of the resolution adopted by the international congress, see pages 109–11.

It is the duty of socialists and organized workers of all countries:

1. To advise and assist the bona fide workingmen immigrants in their first struggles on the new soil; to educate them to the principles of socialism and trade unionism; to receive them in their respective organizations; and to enlist them in the labor movement of the country of their adoption as speedily as possible.

2. To counteract the efforts of misleading representations of capitalist promoters by the publication and wide circulation of truthful reports on the labor conditions of their respective countries, especially through the medium of the International Bureau.

3. To combat with all means at their command the willful importation of cheap foreign labor calculated to destroy labor organizations, to lower the standard of living of the working class, and to retard the ultimate realization of socialism.

4. To seek to procure and protect for all residents in the United States, regardless of race or nativity, full and equal civil and political rights, including the right to naturalization for all and admission on equal terms to the benefits of the schools and other public institutions;

5. To promote the enrollment of workers of alien race or nativity in the political and industrial organization of the working class and the cultivation of a mutual good understanding and fraternal relations between them and the mass of native white workers.

6. By all means to further the assimilation of all such alien elements on a basis of common interest as wageworkers and to rebuke all appeals to racial, national, or religious prejudice against or among them.

The Congress calls upon the socialist representatives in the parliaments of the various countries to introduce legislation along the general lines laid down in this resolution, as well as legislation tending to secure to immigrated workingmen full civil and political rights in the countries of their adoption as speedily as possible. The Congress leaves it to the various national organizations to apply the principles herein announced to the specific needs and conditions of their respective countries.

* * *

LUXEMBURG-LENIN-MARTOV AMENDMENTS
TO MILITARISM RESOLUTION (1907)

The underlined passages below indicate amendments made by Rosa Luxemburg, V. I. Lenin, and Julius Martov that were incorporated into the resolution on militarism and international conflicts approved by the Stuttgart Congress of 1907. On these amendments, Lenin later wrote, "I remember very well that the final drafting of this amendment was preceded by prolonged negotiations between ourselves and Bebel. The first draft made a much more straightforward statement about revolutionary agitation and revolutionary action. When we showed it to Bebel, he replied: 'I cannot accept it, because then the Public Prosecutor will dissolve our party organizations, and we can't have that, as there are no serious developments as yet.' After consultation with legal specialists and numerous redraftings of the text in order to give legal expression to the same idea, a final formula was found which Bebel agreed to accept."[2]

The Congress reaffirms the resolutions passed by previous international congresses against militarism and imperialism, and it again declares that the fight against militarism cannot be separated from the socialist class struggle as a whole.

Wars between capitalist states are as a rule the consequence of their competition in the world market, for every state is eager not only to preserve its markets but also to conquer new ones, principally by the subjugation of foreign nations and the confiscation of their lands. These wars are further engendered by the unceasing and ever-increasing armaments of militarism, which is one of the principal instruments for maintaining bourgeois class rule and for subjugating the working classes politically and economically.

The outbreak of wars is further promoted by the national prejudices systematically cultivated in the interest of the ruling classes, in order to divert the masses of the proletariat from their class duties and international solidarity.

Wars are therefore essential to capitalism; they will not cease until the capitalist system has been done away with, or until the sacrifices in men and money required by the technical development of the military system and the rejection of the armaments race have become so great as to compel the nations to abandon this system.

The working class especially, from which the soldiers are chiefly recruited, and which has to bear the greater part of the financial burdens, is by nature opposed to war, because war is irreconcilable with its aim: the creation of a new economic system founded on a socialist basis and realizing the solidarity of nations.

The Congress therefore considers it to be the duty of the working class, and especially of its parliamentary representatives, to fight with all their might against military and naval armaments, not to grant any money for such purposes, <u>pointing out at the same time the class character of bourgeois society and the real motives for maintaining national antagonisms, and further, to imbue working-class youth with the socialist spirit of universal brotherhood and developing their class consciousness.</u>

The Congress considers that the democratic organization of national defense, by replacing the standing army with the armed people, will prove an effective means for making aggressive wars impossible, and for overcoming national antagonisms.

The International cannot lay down rigid formulas for action by the working class against militarism, as this action must of necessity differ according to the time and conditions of the various national parties. But it is the duty of the International to intensify and coordinate, as much as possible, the efforts of the working class against militarism and war.

In fact, since the Brussels Congress [of 1891], the proletariat in its untiring fight against militarism, by refusing to grant the expenses for military and naval armaments, by democratizing the army, has had recourse, with increasing vigor and success, to the most varied methods of action in order to prevent the outbreak of wars, or to end them, or to make use of the social convulsions caused by war for the emancipation of the working class: as for instance the understanding arrived at between the British and French trade unions after the Fashoda crisis, which served to assure peace and to reestablish friendly relations between Britain and France; the action of the socialist parties in the German and French parliaments during the Morocco crisis: the public demonstrations organized for the same purpose by the French and German socialists; the common action of the Austrian and Italian socialists who met at Trieste in order to ward off a conflict between the two states; further, the vigorous intervention of the socialist workers of Sweden in order to prevent an attack against Norway; and lastly, the heroic sacrifices and fights of the masses of socialist workers and peasants of Russia and Poland rising against the war provoked by the government of the tsar, in order to put an end to it and to make use of the crisis for the emancipation of their country and of the working class. All these efforts show the growing power of the proletariat and its increasing desire to maintain peace by its energetic intervention.

The action of the working classes will be the more successful, the more the mind of the people has been prepared by an unceasing propaganda, and the more the labor parties of the different countries have been spurred on and coordinated by the International.

The Congress further expresses its conviction that under the pressure exerted by the proletariat, the practice of honest arbitration in all disputes will replace the futile attempts of the bourgeois governments, and that in this way the people will be assured of the benefits of universal disarmament, which will allow the enormous resources of energy and money, wasted by armaments and wars, to be applied to the progress of civilization.

In case of war being imminent, the working class and its parliamentary representatives in the countries concerned shall be bound, with the assistance of the International Socialist Bureau, to do all they can to prevent the outbreak of war, using for this purpose the means that appear to them the most effective, and which must naturally vary according to the acuteness of the class struggle and to the general political conditions.

In case war should break out notwithstanding, they shall be bound to intervene for its speedy termination, and to employ all their forces to utilize the economic and political crisis created by the war in order to rouse the masses of the people and thereby hasten the downfall of capitalist class rule.

***

LENIN'S RESOLUTION ON COOPERATIVES (1910)

The following "Draft Resolution of the Social-Democratic Delegation of Russia" was submitted by V. I. Lenin, a member of the Copenhagen Congress's

First Commission. The text is not found in the official congress proceedings, and has been taken from Lenin's article, "The Question of Co-Operative Societies at the International Socialist Congress in Copenhagen."[3]

The Congress is of the opinion:

1. That proletarian consumers' societies improve the situation of the working class in that they reduce the amount of exploitation by all kinds of commercial middlemen, influence the labor conditions of the workers employed by the supplying firms, and improve the situation of their own employees.

2. That these societies can assume great importance for the economic and political mass struggle of the proletariat by supporting the workers during strikes, lockouts, political persecution, etc.

On the other hand the Congress points out:

1. That the improvements that can be achieved with the help of the consumers' societies can only be very inconsiderable as long as the means of production remain in the hands of the class without whose expropriation socialism cannot be attained;

2. That consumers' societies are not organizations for direct struggle against capital and exist alongside similar bodies organized by other classes, which could give rise to the illusion that these organizations are a means by which the social question may be solved without class struggle and the expropriation of the bourgeoisie.

The Congress calls on the workers of all countries:

(a) To join the proletarian consumers' societies and to promote their development in every way, at the same time upholding the democratic character of these organizations;

(b) By untiring socialist propaganda in the consumers' societies, to spread the ideas of class struggle and socialism among the workers;

(c) To strive at the same time to bring about the fullest possible co-operation between all forms of the labor movement.

The Congress also points out that producers' cooperatives can be of importance for the struggle of the working class only if they are a component part of consumers' societies.

NOTES

Introduction

1 No formal name for the Second International existed in the 1889–1914 period. It was usually referred to simply as "the International." The appellation "Second" was meant to distinguish it from the International Workingmen's Association— the First International—which existed from 1864 to 1876.

2 Karl Marx, "On the Hague Congress," in *Marx Engels Collected Works*, vol. 23 (Moscow: Progress Publishers, 1988), 256.

3 Huysmans's estimate on the Second International's strength is quoted in John De Kay, *The Spirit of the International at Berne* (Bern: the author, 1919), 6–7.

4 From Grigorii Zinoviev's report to the Communist International's Second Congress (1920) on conditions for admission to the Third International. In John Riddell, ed., *Workers of the World and Oppressed Peoples, Unite! Proceedings and Documents of the Second Congress, 1920* (New York: Pathfinder Press, 1991), vol. 1, session 6, 294–5 (original pagination).

5 In the Second International's early years, Engels had strongly opposed attempts to create an international center similar to the First International's General Council. He felt that such a move would be premature given the state of the movement at the time, and could lead to nonrevolutionary currents attempting to impose their perspectives on the world movement as a whole. For example, in 1891, on the eve of the Second International's Brussels Congress, Engels wrote, "The Brussels chaps who are, in their heart of hearts, themselves Possibilists [reformists] and have stood by the latter as long as they could, have made a complete *volte-face*; they aim at becoming the General Council of a new International" (letter to Friedrich Adolph Sorge, August 9, 1891, in *Marx Engels Collected Works*, vol. 49, 224). Engels wrote along similar lines in his July 20, 1891, letter to Laura Lafargue (*Collected Works*, vol. 49, 221).

6 Rosa Luxemburg, "Reconstruction of the International," in John Riddell, ed., *Lenin's Struggle for a Revolutionary International: Documents: 1907–1916: The Preparatory Years* (New York: Pathfinder Press, 1984), chapter 4, 187 (original pagination).

7 In his "Notes of a Publicist," Lenin cited Rosa Luxemburg as the author of this metaphor, referring to her alleged words: "Since August 4, 1914, German Social

Democracy has been a stinking corpse." (Lenin, *Collected Works*, vol. 33, 210). Luxemburg never actually wrote those words, however.

Lenin was perhaps referring to the opening lines of Luxemburg's 1915 article, "Rebuilding the International," which he might have been recalling from memory: "On August 4th, 1914, German Social Democracy abdicated politically, and at the same time the Socialist International collapsed." In Robert Looker, ed., *Rosa Luxemburg: Selected Political Writings* (New York: Grove Press, 1974), 197.

Luxemburg also used the corpse analogy elsewhere. For example, her article "Das Versagen der Führer" (the failure of the leaders), published in the January 11, 1919, issue of *Rote Fahne*, stated, "Above all the next time must be devoted to the liquidation of the USPD, this rotting corpse, decayed products of which are poisoning the revolution" (*Gesammelte Werke*, Band 4, 526). In this article, however, Luxemburg was referring to the USPD (Independent Social Democratic Party of Germany), not to German Social Democracy as a whole.

Thanks to Peter Hudis and Paul LeBlanc for research assistance.

8	Following a rally at Haymarket Square in Chicago on May 4, 1886, to support striking workers, a bomb was thrown at police officers by an unknown person, after which the police opened fire on the crowd, killing a number of workers. The incident was used to stage a frame-up against the workers' leaders, who were anarchists. Eight were tried and convicted of murder. Four were hanged, and one committed suicide before his scheduled execution. The Haymarket martyrs were defended and honored by the workers' movement throughout the world, and they became associated with the establishment of May Day as an international workers' holiday.

9	Karl Kautsky, *The Road to Power* (1909), available at Marxists Internet Archive, https://www.marxists.org/archive/kautsky/1909/power/ch01.htm.

10	Karl Marx, "Provisional Rules of the Association," in *Marx Engels Collected Works*, vol. 20 (Moscow: Progress Publishers, 1985), 14.

11	Various translations of the lyrics to "The Internationale" can be found on Marxists Internet Archive, https://www.marxists.org/history/ussr/sounds/lyrics/international.htm.

12	Karl Marx, letter to Ludwig Kugelmann, April 12, 1871, in *Marx Engels Collected Works*, vol. 44 (New York: International Publishers, 1989), 132.

13	Georges Haupt, *La Deuxième Internationale, 1889–1914: étude critique des sources, essai bibliographique* (Paris: Mouton & Co., 1964).

14	A list of the resolutions adopted by the International Socialist Bureau can be found in Haupt, 257–76. See also Haupt, ed., *Bureau Socialiste Internationale*, vol. 1, 1900–1907: *Comptes rendus des réunions, manifestes et circulaires* (Paris and The Hague: Mouton, 1969).

15	The IISG Second International Archives can be accessed at https://search.socialhistory.org/Record/ARCH01299. The Camille Huysmans Archive can be accessed at http://opac.amsab.be/Record/625. The Fonds Georges Haupt can be accessed at http://www.fmsh.fr/fr/diffusion-des-savoirs/29153.

1. Paris Congress, July 14–20, 1889

1   Engels's letters on plans, preparations, and strategic considerations in organizing the 1889 congress can be found in volume 48 of *Marx Engels Collected Works* (New York: International Publishers, 2001).

2   For the Haymarket events, see page 162, note 8.

3   Engels, letter to Friedrich Adolph Sorge, July 17, 1889, in *Marx Engels Collected Works*, vol. 48, 352.

4   An international conference was held at The Hague on February 28, 1889, sponsored by the German Social Democratic Party, in an effort to unite the two rival international labor congresses. The attempt failed, as the Possibilists refused to attend.

The Organizing Committee for the Convocation of an International Working Men's Congress was formed in Paris prior to the 1889 Marxist congress. Its secretaries were Paul Lafargue and Bernard Besset.

5   In 1889 the Swiss government had proposed an international conference to be held in Bern to discuss factory legislation. That initiative was superseded by the Berlin conference of 1890, convened by the German government.

6   Concerning *La Journée de huit heures*, the following is included as an afternote in the French edition of the congress resolutions: "In conformity with the decision taken by the International Socialist Labor Congress, the permanent bureau, at its second session of July 20, designated Switzerland as the site of the executive commission. The delegation of this country has been charged with constituting this commission, to be composed of five members from the same town, which will also be the site of the publication of the journal *La Journée de huit heures*." *International ouvrier socialiste de Paris* (Paris: Imprimerie de la Presse, 1889), 21.

The Zurich executive committee that was charged with overseeing this journal was composed of E. Wullschleger (editor), K. Bürkli, O. Manz, O. Lang, and A. Merk, and backed by the Allgemeiner Schweizerische Gewerkschaftsbund (Swiss General Trade Union Confederation). Planned as a fortnightly, the journal was published in three languages beginning in December 1889: *Der achtstündige Arbeitstag* in German, *La Journée de huit heures* in French, and *the Eight Hours Working Day* in English. The journal ceased publication in early 1891.

7   On May 1, 1886, strikes began in the United States to demand the eight-hour day, with 350,000 workers walking off the job. The strike extended to May 4, when the Haymarket bombing and subsequent police massacre occurred in Chicago.

With this tradition in mind, the third annual convention of the American Federation of Labor, meeting in Saint Louis December 11–15, 1888, voted to set May 1, 1890, as a day for mass meetings in cities throughout the United States in support of the eight-hour day.

2. Brussels Congress, August 16–22, 1891

1   Frederick Engels, letters to Friedrich Adolph Sorge, September 2 and 14, 1891, in *Marx Engels Collected Works*, vol. 49, 232, 238.

2   In *Verhandlungen und Beschlüsse des Internationalen Arbeiterkongresses zu Brüssel* (Berlin: Verlag der Expédition des "Vorwärts," Berliner Volksblatt, 1893), 11. It

is also quoted in J. Lenz, *The Rise and Fall of the Second International* (New York: International Publishers, 1932), 19–20.

3   The Berlin conference of March 15–29, 1890, involving representatives of fourteen European governments, discussed a number of questions related to labor legislation, such as the employment of women and children, Sunday work, mining, and methods of enforcing agreements. Purely advisory in character, the conference helped lead to the formation in 1900 of the International Association for Labor Legislation.

4   The Bordeaux conference took place March 13–20, 1892, attended by two hundred workers. The meeting helped lead to the formation of the Fédération nationale des syndicats maritimes (National Federation of Maritime Unions).

3. Zurich Congress, August 6–12, 1893

1   Engels, "Closing Speech at the International Socialist Workers' Congress in Zurich, August 12, 1893," in *Marx Engels Collected Works*, vol. 27 (Moscow: Progress Publishers, 1990), 404–5.

2   During the summer of 1893, some 250,000 British coal miners were on strike, led by the recently formed Miners' Federation.

3   The Franco-Siamese War of 1893 was sparked by a French effort to undermine British power in the region by spreading its control into Laos, which was controlled by Siamese (Thai) forces. Following the conflict, Laos was ceded to France. The effort nearly escalated into an international incident. Ultimately French-British negotiations established an internationally recognized border between Laos and the British-controlled territory of Upper Burma.

4. London Congress, July 27–August 1, 1896

1   Quoted in Georges Haupt, *La Deuxième Internationale, 1889–1914: étude critique des sources, essay bibliographique* (Paris: Mouton & Co., 1964), 150.

2   *International Socialist Workers and Trade Union Congress, London 1896* (London: Twentieth Century Press Limited, n.d.), 7.

3   The draft resolution on education and physical development presented to the congress included as point 2 the following: "That the school arrangements should include one meal a day in common as in the *cantines scolaires*, without invidious distinction between rich and poor; and that adequate provision be made for the complete maintenance and education, according to the best methods, of all orphan or destitute children," quoted in *International Socialist Workers and Trade Union Congress, London 1896*, 35–39. This was deleted following an amendment proposed by Edith Lanchester and Mary Gray and approved by the congress, and the subsequent points were renumbered.

4   Presumably a reference to the Berlin conference of 1890. See page 163, note 5.

5   Resolutions 7 and 8 on international organization are not included in the official record and have not been located for this volume.

6   The published proceedings of the 1896 London Congress say the following concerning the resolution on international organization: "Owing to the prohibitive laws in general continental States against international combination, recommendations 1, 2, and 3 were finally abandoned after having been passed by the

congress." See *Full Report of the Proceedings of the International Workers' Congress, London, July and August 1896* (London, "The Labour Leader," n.d.), 39.

7   The truck system refers to capitalists paying workers in company scrip, rather than money.

8   Concerning the miscellaneous resolutions, the published proceedings state here that "the President to save time put the resolution which was carried by acclamation. He then put the first three paragraphs of the report, which were carried unanimously. As to the fourth paragraph the President pointed out that it was impossible considering how late it was to carry out the suggestion made in it." See *International Socialist Workers and Trade Union Congress, London 1896*, 51.

9   In 1896 Gustave Delory was elected mayor of Lille, becoming the first socialist mayor in France.

10 In July 1896 Justice William Grantham presided over a lawsuit by a London piano maker alleging that picketing strikers had made it impossible for him to practice his trade, and were in violation of the Conspiracy and Protection of Property Act of 1875. Justice Grantham issued instructions to the jury that by picketing the strikers were doing something "they have no right to do by law." The jury found for the manufacturer and awarded him damages.

11 Up to ten Russian delegates attended the 1896 London Congress, headed by Georgy V. Plekhanov.

12 In July 1896 riots directed at Italian immigrant workers erupted in Zurich, Switzerland, with a number of the immigrants' homes destroyed. In the wake of this violence, some 1,500 Italian families were evicted from their homes, and 6,000 Italian workers were forced to leave the area.

13 A reference to the founding meeting of what was to become the International Workingmen's Association (the First International), held in London on September 28, 1864.

14 A war for Cuba's independence from Spain began in 1895, coming after earlier wars in 1868–1878 and 1879–1880. By 1898 Spain was bogged down by the independence forces, but following the Spanish-American War Cuba fell under US domination.

In 1895 an independence rebellion began in Crete, then a possession of the Ottoman Empire. Crete became independent in 1898. In 1908 it declared union with Greece.

Macedonia, then under Ottoman control, was the scene of an 1893–1908 war conducted primarily between Greek and Bulgarian forces.

5. Paris Congress, September 23–27, 1900

1   Eduard Bernstein, *Evolutionary Socialism: A Criticism and Affirmation* (New York: Schocken Books, 1961), 202.

2   Kautsky spelled out this intention in a speech he delivered at the German Social Democratic Party's 1903 congress in Dresden: "Back then [in 1900] I tried to formulate the resolution in such a way that it went against Millerand in principle, but presented his behavior as a mistake rather than a crime. I wanted to preserve the principled standpoint, and yet pave the way for unity among the French. My latter efforts were in vain. . . . I thereby position myself against the view put forward by the revisionists that we will come to power by conquering

one political ministry after another, and that therefore we can take power piecemeal, without a revolution." Kautsky's words are quoted from *Protokoll über die Verhandlungen des Parteitages der Sozialdemokratischen Partei Deutschlands, Abgehalten zu Dresden, vom 13. bis 20. September 1903* (Berlin: Verlag Expedition der Buchhandlung Vorwärts, 1903), 384. Thanks to Sean Larson and Ben Lewis for research assistance.

3   Finland and a large portion of Poland were part of the tsarist empire, and were increasingly subject to Russification and other oppressive measures.

4   The war in South Africa (known commonly as the Second Boer War) was fought from October 1899 to May 1902 between British troops and forces of the South African Republic (Transvaal) and the Orange Free State. In this war, the British Empire sent almost half a million troops in an effort to strengthen its influence in southern Africa. Given Britain's military superiority, the Boer forces relied primarily on guerrilla tactics. British forces responded with extreme brutality, herding civilian farmers into concentration camps, where many died.

5   A nationalist movement in Armenia, part of the Ottoman Empire, had developed during the 1870s. In 1894–1896 a pogrom was carried out by the Ottoman government, leading to the massacre of up to several hundred thousand Armenians.

6   The International Federation of Ship, Dock and River Workers was founded in 1896. In 1898 the federation changed its name to the International Transport Workers' Federation, which continues to exist.

7   The term "municipal socialism" arose in Britain in the 1870s to describe social reforms undertaken by local governments. By the 1890s this perspective was widely propagated in Britain, the US, Germany, and elsewhere.

8   Concerning point (b) of the resolution on municipal socialism, the following sentence was included in the version of this resolution published in the *Social-Democrat*: "This paragraph was eventually deleted as the International Committee formed in accordance with the first resolution [on international organization] has charge of collecting all documents relating to municipal life," *Social-Democrat* 4, no. 11 (November 15, 1900): 342–43.

9   For the 1893 Zurich resolution, see page 46. There was no such resolution at the 1889 Paris Congress. The London Congress of 1896 did not in fact adopt a resolution on the general strike, although it did reject a resolution on it by the minority of the Economic and Industrial Commission.

6. Amsterdam Congress, August 14–20, 1904

1   For Van Kol's remarks about a socialist state and colonies, see *Sixième congrès socialiste international tenu à Amsterdam du 14 au 20 août 1904* (Brussels: Gand, Imprimerie Coopérative "Volksdrukkerij," 1904), 44. In German, *Internationaler Sozialistenkogress zu Amsterdam, 14. bis 20. August 1904* (Berlin: Verlag der Expedition der Buchhandlung Vorwärts, 1904), 23.

2   For Luxemburg's amendment, see *Sixième congrès socialiste international tenu à Amsterdam du 14 au 20 août 1904*, 148.

3   A series of strikes and labor battles were waged in Colorado by the Western Federation of Miners in 1903 and 1904, involving gold and silver miners, as well as other mill workers.

4   Some 1,500 Italian working people were sentenced to prison following a popular uprising that took place in Milan, Italy, in May 1898, which broke out after government troops opened fire on demonstrators protesting skyrocketing food prices. Several hundred people were killed. The Comitato Pro Vittime Politiche (Committee in Support of Political Victims) campaigned for the imprisoned victims. Most of the sentences were eventually commuted.

5   Hungary was then a part of the Austro-Hungarian Empire. The socialist movement within the empire was organized federally, and the Hungarian socialists had their own structure and organization.

6   The war between Russia and Japan, which grew out of a rivalry for dominance in Korea and Manchuria, lasted from February 1904 to September 1905. It ended in a victory for Japan.

7   The German-language proceedings (*Internationaler Sozialistenkogress zu Amsterdam, 14. bis 20. August 1904*) refer to the passage of the resolution on anti-Semitic persecution in Russia on page 44. The French-language proceedings (*Sixième congrès socialiste international tenu à Amsterdam du 14 au 20 août 1904*) refer to it on page 94.

8   Translated here from the Yiddish by Myra Mniewski.

9   The Pale of Settlement was an area in the western region of the tsarist empire where Jews were legally compelled to live, being forbidden to live outside of it. Even within this region, Jews were often barred from living in certain cities or towns. The borders of what became the Pale of Settlement first began to be established in the 1790s. The restrictions were not abolished until the Russian Revolution of 1917.

10   As social tensions rose in Russia on the eve of the 1905 revolution, a wave of anti-Semitic pogroms was organized by monarchist elements, with the support and complicity of the tsarist regime. Several thousand Jews were killed in these murderous onslaughts during the 1903–1906 period. In addition, thousands of Jews were expelled from towns and cities.

      The Kishinev pogrom of April 1903, in particular, received wide coverage in the world press, provoking an international outcry. On May 20, 1903, the International Socialist Bureau issued a manifesto about the Kishinev pogrom. For the text, see Haupt, ed., *Bureau Socialiste Internationale, vol. 1 1900–1907: Comptes rendus des réunions, manifestes et circulaires* (Paris and The Hague: Mouton, 1969), 75–76.

7. Stuttgart Congress, August 18–24, 1907

1   Riddell, ed., *Lenin's Struggle for a Revolutionary International*, chapter 1, 17–18 (original pagination).

2   At the 1907 Stuttgart Congress, for the first time, the different delegations were entitled to a number of votes in accordance with the strength of the parties they represented. The largest received twenty votes, the smaller ones from fifteen down to two.

3   A reference to the resolutions on international organization adopted by the London and Paris Congresses. See pages 54–55 and 68–69.

4   The Fashoda Incident of September 18, 1898, was the climax of a series of territorial disputes between the British and French colonial empires in Africa.

It involved a military standoff between British and French troops in Fashoda in Egyptian Sudan. Following the incident, the two powers eventually came to an agreement on the boundaries of their respective spheres of influence.

5   In April 1904 the French and British governments formed the Entente Cordiale to advance their respective interests in North Africa; France subsequently signed a secret treaty with Spain to partition Morocco. The German rulers, however, had their own designs, and declared for Moroccan independence, leading to the First Moroccan Crisis of 1905–1906 and sparking the threat of war between Germany and France. The crisis was resolved at a conference in Algeciras, which acknowledged Germany's economic interests while entrusting France and Spain with policing Morocco.

Socialists in Germany and France organized protest meetings and demonstrations against the war threat. A public meeting organized by the SPD in Berlin on July 9, 1905, for example, had invited French Socialist Party leader Jean Jaurès to speak. The latter's participation in the meeting, however, was prohibited by Germany's chancellor.

6   On May 21–22, 1905, a summit meeting was held in Trieste between Italian and Austrian socialist leaders, headed by Leonida Bissolati and Victor Adler, to discuss a coordinated response in case war broke out between the two countries.

7   In 1905 mass working-class mobilizations in Sweden helped prevent a war by that country's ruling class against Norway following the Norwegian declaration of independence from Sweden.

8   The social crisis resulting from the Russo-Japanese War of 1904–1905 was a factor leading to the outbreak of the revolution of 1905 throughout the tsarist empire.

9   The Brussels conference of May 27–28, 1899, attended by labor and socialist delegations from eleven countries, laid down a set of conditions for participation in the Second International's Paris Congress of 1900. The congress would be open to all political organizations whose object was to replace the capitalist mode of production and property with socialist ones and that recognized the need for political action. All trade unions standing on the ground of the class struggle and recognizing legislative and parliamentary action as one of the means to this end were also invited.

10 The International Secretariat of National Trade Union Centers, linked politically to the Second International, was founded in 1901. Its affiliates included the national union federations in Britain, Belgium, Denmark, Finland, Germany, Norway, and Sweden. Its offices were moved to Berlin in 1903. In 1913 the organization changed its name to the International Federation of Trade Unions.

11 The Romanian Peasants' Revolt of February–April 1907 was an uprising throughout Romania against the country's semifeudal system of land ownership. Some 140,000 troops were mobilized to suppress the revolt, with up to 11,000 peasants killed.

12 On August 5–7, 1907, French forces carried out a naval bombardment of Casablanca, killing up to seven thousand Moroccan residents. The effort marked the beginning of the French conquest of Morocco. The Spanish government gave its support to the French attack, sending a gunship and a small number of troops.

13 In February 1906, three leaders of the Western Federation of Miners—William ("Big Bill") Haywood, Charles Moyer, and George Pettibone—were arrested in Denver, Colorado, and extradited to Idaho, charged with having assassinated the governor of Idaho two months earlier. The frame-up was conducted in an obvious attempt to break the union. Facing the death penalty, Haywood was acquitted in July 1907. Tried separately, Pettibone was also found not guilty, after which charges against Moyer were dropped.

8. Copenhagen Congress, August 28–September 3, 1910

1   For the Haymarket martyrs, see page 162, note 8. For the judicial frame-up of miners' leaders Haywood, Pettibone, and Moyer, see page 168, note 13.

2   Francisco Ferrer, a Catalan educator and anarchist, was arrested in September 1909, in the wake of the July 1909 Tragic Week events in Barcelona (see page 170, note 13). Found guilty by a military tribunal as the "author and leader of the rebellion," he was executed by firing squad on October 13, 1909.

3   On April 23–26, 1905, a unity congress was held in Paris between the two principal organizations of French socialism—the Parti socialiste français led by Jean Jaurès and the Parti socialiste de France led by Jules Guesde. The new united organization was formally named the Section française de l'Internationale ouvrière (French Section of the Workers International, SFIO) but was known generally as the French Socialist Party. The impetus for the unification came from the resolution on party unity adopted by the 1904 Amsterdam Congress.

4   The Danish lockout of 1899, organized by the employers' association, lasted more than three months and affected about 20 percent of the country's nonagricultural labor force.

    In June–July 1909, Swedish employers began a series of lockouts as they sought to impose wage cuts. In response, workers organized a monthlong general strike of 300,000 workers in August–September of that year.

    In Germany, there were 1,121 lockouts in 1910. At one point, 217,000 workers were locked out at the same time.

5   The truck system refers to capitalists paying workers in company scrip, rather than money.

6   The Bern conference of September 1906, composed of officials from fourteen countries, was called to sign an agreement on labor legislation discussed at a conference in Bern the previous year.

    For the 1890 Berlin conference, see page 163, note 5.

7   Julius Wezosal, editor of *Proletareets*, the Latvian-language organ of the US Socialist Labor Party, had been accused by the tsarist government in Russia of having participated in a robbery of the Russian treasury in Tiflis during the 1905 revolution, even though he was in Switzerland at the time. Wezosal was arrested and imprisoned in Boston in 1910, and was subject to extradition proceedings by US authorities. With legal assistance from the Political Refugees' Defense League, Wezosal was able to win his case the following year.

8   In March 1910 Vinayak Damodar Savarkar was arrested in London by British police as a result of an antigovernment speech he had given in Mumbai, India, in 1906. As Savarkar was transported back to India for trial, on July 7 he escaped when his ship reached Marseilles, France. The following day French

police arrested him and handed him back over to British authorities. At his trial, Savarkar was sentenced to fifty years' imprisonment. He was released in 1924.

9   For an account of the debate in the Commission on Cooperatives, see Lenin, "The Question of Co-operative Societies at the International Socialist Congress in Copenhagen," in Lenin, *Collected Works* (Moscow: Progress Publishers, 1960–1971), vol. 16, 275–83. In the article Lenin tells of his decision to vote in favor of the resolution at the congress plenary.

10   The two best-known cases illustrating the Japanese government's efforts to suppress the socialist and labor movements at the time were, firstly, the June 1908 arrests of fourteen socialists as a result of the June 1908 "Red Flag Riot"; at their trial each defendant was sentenced to prison terms of one to two and a half years. Secondly, in May 1910 twenty-six socialists and anarchists were arrested and accused of plotting to assassinate the emperor. Following a frame-up trial in January 1911, twenty-four were sentenced to death. Twelve had their sentences commuted to life in prison, and twelve were hanged.

11   In May 1910, in response to a threatened general strike, the Argentine government unleashed a wave of repression, closing most union headquarters and jailing and deporting scores of workers' leaders.

12   In July 1908 the Young Turk movement became the dominant power in the Ottoman Empire, restoring the 1876 constitution, recalling parliament, and establishing a constitutional monarchy with a program of constitutional rule and modernization. On April 25, 1909, the Turkish government imposed martial law; this was followed up by decreeing a new labor law on August 9 of that year prohibiting unions in public service and severely limiting all strikes.

13   The Tragic Week events in July–August 1909 involved a series of semi-insurrectional battles pitting thousands of workers in Barcelona and other cities of Catalonia against Spanish troops. The rebellion was sparked by the call-up of reserve troops for Spain's colonial war in Morocco. Up to 150 people were reported killed, and 1,700 were indicted for rebellion in military courts. Five were sentenced to death and executed.

14   In May 1910 Socialist Party leader Pablo Iglesias became the first Spanish SP member elected to parliament, from Madrid. For the execution of Ferrer, see page 169, note 2.

15   In late 1905, the Constitutional Revolution began in Iran, then under the rule of the Qajar dynasty. The revolution established a parliamentary body, the Majlis. In response to the revolutionary upsurge, Britain and Russia, the two main colonial powers in the region, signed the Anglo-Russian Convention on August 31, 1907, dividing Iran into spheres of influence: Britain's sphere of influence was in the south, Russia's in the center and north. Russia, strongly opposed to the Constitutional Revolution, supported a coup to restore full monarchical rule in June 1908. Opposition to the coup was strongest in the area around Tabriz. In early 1909, Russia sent troops to the cities of Tabriz, Rasht, and Qazvin attempting to restore order.

16   The Armenian Revolutionary Federation—the Dashnaktsutyun—was founded in 1890, becoming the leading Armenian national organization. Its branch in Tabriz joined in the Constitutional Revolution, and was subject to Russian repression. The tsarist government was especially fearful of the Armenian

nationalists' alignment with the Young Turk movement and its liberalizing influence. In 1903 the Dashnaktsutyun added the struggle against tsarism into its program.

17   Kurdish political organization within the Ottoman Empire was dominated by landowning tribal chiefs, which gave Kurdish village society a semifeudal character.

18   During the 1890s, armed confrontations had developed between Kurdish and Armenian forces within the Ottoman Empire. The tsarist regime in Russia hoped to use the Armenian national movement to undermine the Ottoman Empire. M. N. Charykov (1855–1930) was Russia's ambassador in Constantinople from 1909 to 1912.

19   A Russian protectorate since 1809, Finland had been allowed its own constitution and laws. In 1903, however, the tsarist regime began stripping Finland of these rights, revoking the Finnish constitution. The 1905 revolution in Russia gave rise to an upsurge in Finnish nationalist activity, which led the tsarist regime to authorize the election of a unicameral assembly in Finland. In June 1910, however, the Russian Duma enacted a new law giving the Russian Imperial Council effective control over Finland's internal administration.

9. Basel Congress, November 24–25, 1912

1   Lenin, "Opportunism and the Collapse of the Second International," in Lenin, *Collected Works*, vol. 22, 110.

2   The First Balkan War, from October to December 1912, was waged by Serbia, Bulgaria, Greece, and Montenegro against the Ottoman Empire. Under the terms of a May 1913 peace treaty, the Ottoman Empire lost almost all its remaining European territory. A Second Balkan War was waged from June to August 1913 with Serbia and Greece defeating Bulgaria over division of the territory conquered from the Ottoman Empire in Macedonia.

3   The defeat of France in the Franco-Prussian War of 1870–1871 helped lead to the Paris Commune of March–May 1871, the first historical experience of a revolutionary working-class government.

Afterword: 1914

1   Kautsky, "Internationalism and the War," in Riddell, ed. *Lenin's Struggle for a Revolutionary International,* chapter 4, 147–48 (original pagination).

2   Branting's speech can be found in De Kay, *The Spirit of the International at Berne*, 17.

3   From "Manifesto of the Communist International to the Proletariat of the Entire World," in John Riddell, ed., *Founding the Communist International: Proceedings and Documents of the First Congress: March 1919* (New York: Pathfinder Press, 1987), 230–31 (original pagination).

4   "Preface to the Fourth German Edition of the *Manifesto of the Communist Party*," in *Marx Engels Collected Works*, vol. 27, 60.

Appendixes

1   A general strike in Belgium April 12–18, 1893, called by the Belgian Workers Party under pressure from miners, was observed by 200,000 workers. Fearing a full-scale revolution, the government sent in the military and a number of strikers were killed. Eventually caving in to the pressure, the Belgian parliament introduced numerous electoral reforms that led to the establishment of universal male suffrage.

2   Lenin, "On the Amendment to Bebel's Resolution at the Stuttgart Congress," in Lenin, *Collected Works*, vol. 36, 415.

3   Lenin, *Collected Works*, vol. 16, 278–79.

SOURCES FOR RESOLUTIONS

Below is a listing of the sources used for each resolution in the three official languages of the Second International. IISG refers to the Internationaal Instituut voor Sociale Geschiedenis (International Institute of Social History), repository of the Second International Archives.

1. PARIS CONGRESS OF 1889

Official proceedings for this congress were published in German only: *Protokoll des Internationalen Arbeiter-Congresses zu Paris. Abgehalten vom 14. bis 20. Juli 1889* (Nürnberg: Druck und Verlag von Worlein & Comp., 1890), hereafter *Protokoll 1889*. Most resolutions were published in French in *Congrès International ouvrier socialiste de Paris* (Paris: Imprimerie de la Presse, 1889), hereafter *CIOSP*. For the specific resolutions:

Unity of the Socialist Movement and International Congresses
In German, *Protokoll 1889*, p. 16. For this book, translated from the German.

International Labor Legislation
In French, *CIOSP*, pp. 18–19. In German, *Protokoll 1889*, pp. 121–22. For this book, translated from the French.

Ways and Means for Winning Demands
In French, *CIOSP*, pp.19–20 and 21. In German, *Protokoll 1889*, pp. 120–21. For this book, translated from the French.

International Demonstration on May 1, 1890
In English, *Monthly Labor Review* 9, no. 2, August 1919, p. 47. In French, *CIOSP*, pp. 20–21. In German, *Protokoll 1889*, p. 123.

Abolition of Standing Armies / General Arming of the Population
In English, *Bulletin Périodique du Bureau Socialiste International*, no. 9, p. 3, n.d. In French, *CIOSP*, pp. 21–22. In German, *Protokoll 1889*, pp. 119–20.

Political and Economic Action

In French, *CIOSP*, p. 23. In German, *Protokoll 1889*, pp. 124–25. The original English text has not been located. For this book, translated from the French.

2. BRUSSELS CONGRESS OF 1891

Official proceedings: In French, *Congrès international ouvrier socialiste tenu à Bruxelles du 16 au 23 août 1891* (Brussels: Imprimerie Désiré Brismée, 1893), hereafter *Compte rendu 1891*. In German, *Verhandlungen und Beschlüsse des Internationalen Arbeiter-Kongresses zu Brüssel* (Berlin: Verlag der Expédition des "Vorwärts," Berliner Volksblatt, 1893), hereafter *Protokoll 1891*. For the specific resolutions:

Conditions of Admission to the Congress

In German, *Protokoll 1891*, p. 5. In French, *Compte rendu 1891*, p. 14. For this book, translated from the German.

Labor Legislation

In English, The *Times* (London), "Socialist Labour Congress in Brussels," August 20, 1891. In French, *Compte rendu 1891*, pp. 39–40. In German, *Protokoll 1891*, pp. 8–9.

Working-Class Organization and Action

In English, *Second International Archives*, IISG. In French, *Compte rendu 1891*, pp. 60–61. In German, *Protokoll 1891*, pp. 23–24.

Piecework

In French, *Compte rendu 1891*, pp. 81–82. In German, *Protokoll 1891*, pp. 31–32. For this book, translated from the French.

International First of May Demonstrations

In English, *Second International Archives*, IISG. In French, *Compte rendu 1891*, p. 89. In German, *Protokoll 1891*, p. 33.

Women's Equality

In English, *The Times* (London), August 24, 1891. *Second International Archives*, IISG. In French, *Compte rendu 1891*, p. 85. In German, *Protokoll 1891*, p. 32.

The Jewish Question

In French, *Compte rendu 1891*, pp. 43–44. In German, *Protokoll 1891*, p. 16. For this book, translated from the French.

Militarism

In English, *Bulletin Périodique du Bureau Socialiste International*, no. 9, p. 4, n.d. In French, *Compte rendu 1891*, pp. 64–65. In German, *Protokoll 1891*, p. 26.

Motion on Maritime Workers

In French, *Compte rendu 1891*, p. 93. For this book, translated from the French.

3. ZURICH CONGRESS OF 1893

Official proceedings: *Protokoll des Internationalen Sozialistischen Arbeiterkongresses in der Tonhalle Zürich vom 6. bis 12. August 1893* (Zurich: Buchhandlung des Schweiz, Grütlivereins, 1894), hereafter *Protokoll 1893*. For the specific resolutions:

Conditions of Admission to the Congress

In English, *Full Report of the Proceedings of the International Workers' Congress, London, July and August 1896* (London, "The Labour Leader," n.d.), p. 7. In German, *Protokoll 1893*, pp. 5, 6.

The Eight-Hour Day

In German, *Protokoll 1893*, p 19. For this book, translated from the German.

Political Action

In German, *Protokoll 1893*, pp. 40–41. For this book, translated from the German.

The Agrarian Question

In English and French, *Second International Archives*, IISG. In German, *Protokoll 1893*, pp. 48.

National and International Organization of Trade Unions

In English and French *Second International Archives*, IISG. In German, *Protokoll 1893*, p. 49–50.

Common Action with Regard to First of May Demonstration

In English and French, *Second International Archives*, IISG. In German, *Protokoll 1893*, pp. 35–36.

Protective Legislation for Working Women

In English and French, *Second International Archives*, IISG. In German, *Protokoll 1893*, pp. 36–37.

Social Democracy in the Event of War

In English and French, *Bulletin Périodique du Bureau Socialiste International*, no. 9, p. 4, n.d. In German, *Protokoll 1893*, p. 20.

International Organization of Social Democracy

In English and French, *Second International Archives*, IISG. In German, *Protokoll 1893*, p. 54.

The General Strike

In English and French, *Second International Archives*, IISG. In German, *Protokoll 1893*, pp. 53–54.

Universal Suffrage

In German, *Protokoll 1893*, p. 52. For this book, translated from the German.

Solidarity with British Miners

In German, *Protokoll 1893*, p. 12. For this book, translated from the German.

Motion on French and Siamese Crisis

In German, *Protokoll* 1893, p. 13. For this book, translated from the German.

4. LONDON CONGRESS OF 1896

Official proceedings: In English, *International Socialist Workers and Trade Union Congress. London 1896* (London: Twentieth Century Press Limited, n.d.), hereafter *ISWTUC 1896*. In German, *Verhandlungen und Beschlüsse des Internationalen Sozialistischen Arbeiter- und Gewerkschafts-Kongresses zu London vom 27. July bis 1. August 1896* (Berlin: Verlag der Expedition der Buchhandlung Vorwärts, 1896), hereafter *Protokoll 1896*. In French, some of the material is found in *Congrès international socialiste des travailleurs et des chambres syndicales ouvrières: Londres 26 juillet–2 août 1896* (Geneva: Minkoff Reprint, 1980). For the specific resolutions:

The Agrarian Question

In English, *ISWTUC 1896*, pp. 25–26. In German, *Protokoll 1896*, pp. 13–14. In French, *Second International Archives*, IISG.

Political Action

In English, *ISWTUC 1896*, pp. 30–31. In German, *Protokoll 1896*, pp. 17–18. In French, *Second International Archives*, IISG.

Education and Physical Development

In English, *ISWTUC 1896*, pp. 35–36. In German, *Protokoll 1896*, pp. 20–22. In French, *Second International Archives*, IISG.

International Organization

In English, *ISWTUC 1896*, pp. 40–41. In German, *Protokoll 1896*, pp. 23–24. In French, *Second International Archives*, IISG.

War and Militarism

In English, *ISWTUC 1896*, pp. 41–42. In German, *Protokoll 1896*, p. 24. In French, *Second International Archives*, IISG.

The Economic and Industrial Question

In English, *ISWTUC 1896*, pp. 46–48. In German, *Protokoll 1896*, pp. 27–29. In French, *Second International Archives*, IISG.

Miscellaneous Resolutions

In English, *ISWTUC 1896*, p. 51. In German, *Protokoll 1896*, p. 30. In French, *Second International Archives*, IISG.

The Next Congress
In English, *ISWTUC 1896*, p. 52. In German, *Protokoll 1896*, p. 30. In French, *Second International Archives*, IISG.

Solidarity with Socialist Mayor of Lille
In English, *ISWTUC 1896*, p. 25. In German, *Protokoll 1896*, p. 13.

Protest against Antilabor Ruling
In English, *ISWTUC 1896*, p. 29. In German, *Protokoll 1896*, p. 16.

The Fight against Russian Tsarism
In English, *ISWTUC 1896*, pp. 29–30. In German, *Protokoll 1896*, pp. 16–17.

Greetings to Bulgarian Social Democrats
In English, *ISWTUC 1896*, p. 45. In German, *Protokoll 1896*, p. 26.

Violence against Immigrant Workers
In English, *ISWTUC 1896*, p. 45. In German, *Protokoll 1896*, p. 26.

Remembrance of First International
In English, *ISWTUC 1896*, p. 45.

Solidarity with Cuba, Crete, and Macedonia
In English, *ISWTUC 1896*, p. 51.

5. PARIS CONGRESS OF 1900

Official proceedings: In French, *Cinquième congrès socialiste international tenu à Paris du 23 au 27 Septembre 1900* (Paris, Société Nouvelle de Librairie et d'Édition, 1901), hereafter *Compte rendu 1900*. In German, *Internationaler Sozialisten-Kongress zu Paris, 23. bis 27. September 1900* (Berlin: Verlag der Expedition der Buchhandlung Vorwärts, 1900), hereafter *Protokoll 1900*. For the specific resolutions:

International Organization
In English, *The Social-Democrat* (London) 4, no. 11, November 15, 1900, pp. 338–39. In French, *Compte rendu 1900*, pp. 101–2. In German, *Protokoll 1900*, p. 10.

Workday Limits and Minimum Wage
In English, *The Social-Democrat* (London) 4, no. 11, November 15, 1900, p. 339. In French, *Compte rendu 1900*, p. 103. In German, *Protokoll 1900*, pp. 13–14.

Emancipation of Labor and Expropriation of the Bourgeoisie
In English, *The Social-Democrat* (London) 4, no. 11, November 15, 1900, pp. 339–40. In French, *Compte rendu 1900*, pp. 104–5. In German, *Protokoll 1900*, pp. 15.

The Fight against Militarism and War

In English, *The Social-Democrat* (London) 4, no. 11, November 15, 1900, p. 340. In French, *Compte rendu 1900*, pp. 105–6. In German, *Protokoll 1900*, pp. 27–28.

Colonial Policy

In English, *The Social-Democrat* (London) 4, no. 11, November 15, 1900, p. 341. In French, *Compte rendu 1900*, pp. 106–7. In German, *Protokoll 1900*, pp. 25–26.

Organization of Maritime Workers

In English, The *Social-Democrat* (London) 4, no. 11, November 15, 1900, pp. 341–42. In French, *Compte rendu 1900*, pp. 107–11. In German, *Protokoll 1900*, p. 29.

Universal Suffrage and Popular Sovereignty

In English, *The Social-Democrat* (London) 4, no. 11, November 15, 1900, p. 342. In French, *Compte rendu 1900*, pp. 111–12. In German, *Protokoll 1900*, pp. 29–30.

Municipal Socialism

In English, *The Social-Democrat* (London) 4, no. 11, November 15, 1900, pp. 342–43. In French, *Compte rendu 1900*, pp. 112–14. In German, *Protokoll 1900*, p. 30.

Socialists in Public Office and Alliances with Bourgeois Parties (Kautsky Resolution)

In English, *The Social-Democrat* (London) 4, no. 11, November 15, 1900, pp. 343–44. In French, *Compte rendu 1900*, pp. 114–16. In German, *Protokoll 1900*, p. 17.

The First of May

In English, *The Social-Democrat* (London) 4, no. 11, November 15, 1900, p. 344. In French, *Compte rendu 1900*, p. 116. In German, *Protokoll 1900*, p. 14.

Trusts

In English, *The Social-Democrat* (London) 4, no. 11, November 15, 1900, pp. 344–45. In French, *Compte rendu 1900*, pp. 116–18. In German, *Protokoll 1900*, p. 31.

The General Strike

In English, *The Social-Democrat* (London) 4, no. 11, November 15, 1900, p. 346. In French, *Compte rendu 1900*, p. 118. In German, *Protokoll 1900*, p. 32.

6. AMSTERDAM CONGRESS OF 1904

Official proceedings: In German, *Internationaler Sozialisten-Kongress zu Amsterdam, 14. bis 20. August 1904* (Berlin: Verlag der Expedition der

Buchhandlung Vorwärts, 1904), hereafter *Protokoll 1904*. In French, *Sixième congrès socialiste international tenu à Amsterdam du 14 au 20 août 1904* (Brussels: Gand, Imprimerie Coopérative "Volksdrukkerij," 1904), hereafter *Compte rendu 1904*. A number of English-language texts can be found in Daniel De Leon, *Flashlights of the Amsterdam Congress, 1904* (New York: New York Labor News Company, n.d.), hereafter *Flashlights 1904*. For the specific resolutions:

On Tactics (Dresden-Amsterdam Resolution)

In English, *International Socialist Review* 5, no. 3, September 1904, pp. 170–71. Also, *Flashlights 1904*, pp. 96–97. In German, *Protokoll 1904*, pp. 31–32. In French, *Compte rendu 1904*, pp 114–67.

Party Unity

In English, *International Socialist Review* 5, no. 4, October 1904, p. 231. Also, *Flashlights 1904*, pp. 102–3. In German, *Protokoll 1904*, p. 32. In French, *Compte rendu 1904*, pp. 112–13.

The General Strike

In English, *Second International Archives*, IISG. Also, *Flashlights 1904*, pp. 98–99. In German, *Protokoll 1904*, pp. 24–25. In French, *Compte rendu 1904*, pp. 45–46.

The First of May

In English, *International Socialist Review* 5, no. 4, October 1904, pp. 231–32. In German, *Protokoll 1904*, pp. 53–54. In French, *Compte rendu 1904*, pp. 126.

Workers' Insurance

In English, *International Socialist Review* 5, no. 3, September 1904, pp. 171–72. In German, *Protokoll 1904*, p. 15. In French, *Compte rendu 1904*, pp. 29–30.

Trusts

In English, *Second International Archives*, IISG. Also, *International Socialist Review* 5, no. 4, October 1904, p. 232. In German, *Protokoll 1904*, pp. 54–55. In French, *Compte rendu 1904*, pp. 124–25.

Colonial Policy

In English, *The Comrade* 13, no. 13, October 1904, p. 271. In German, *Protokoll 1904*, pp. 23–24. In French, *Compte rendu 1904*, pp. 42–43.

On British India

In English, *The Comrade* 3, no. 13, October 1904, p. 271. Also, *International Socialist Review* 5, no. 3, *September* 1904, p. 174. Also, *Second International Archives*, IISG. In German, *Protokoll 1904*, pp. 19–20. In French, *Compte rendu 1904*, p. 36.

Support for Miners of Colorado

In English, *Second International Archives*, IISG. In German, *Protokoll 1904*, p. 13. In French, *Compte rendu 1904*, pp. 26–27.

Solidarity with Italian Prisoners

In English, *Second International Archives*, IISG. In German, *Protokoll 1904*, p. 22. In French, *Compte rendu 1904*, p. 41.

Universal Women's Suffrage

In German, *Protokoll 1904*, p. 54. In French, *Compte rendu 1904*, pp. 125–26. For this book, translated from the German.

On Hungary

In French, *Compte rendu 1904*, pp. 122–23. In German, *Protokoll 1904*, p. 53. For this book, translated from the French.

The Russo-Japanese War

In German, *Protokoll 1904*, p. 10. In French, *Compte rendu 1904*, p. 23. For this book, translated from the French.

Anti-Semitic Persecution in Russia

For this book, translated from the Yiddish. In Moshe Rafes and Avraham Kirzshnits, eds., *Der Yidisher arbetyer*, vol. 2, pt. 1 (Moscow 1925), p. 100.

Support for Russian Proletariat

In German, *Protokoll 1904*, p. 50. In French, *Compte rendu 1904*, p. 117. For this book, translated from the French.

7. STUTTGART CONGRESS OF 1907

Official proceedings: In German, *Internationaler Sozialisten-Kongress, Stuttgart 1907, vom 18. bis 24. August 1907* (Berlin: Verlag Buchhandlung Vorwärts, 1907), hereafter *Protokoll 1907*. In French, *VIIe Congrès Socialiste International tenu à Stuttgart du 16 au 24 août 1907* (Brussels: Imprimerie-Lithographie Veuve Désiré Brismée, 1908), hereafter *Compte rendu 1907*. Draft resolutions published by International Socialist Bureau: *Propositions et projets de résolutions avec rapports explicatifs présentés au Congrès socialiste international de Stuttgart (18–24 août 1907) / Anträge und Beschlussentwürfe nebst Begründungen an den Internationalen Sozialistischen Kongress zu Stuttgart (18–24 August 1907) / Proposals and Drafts of Resolutions with Explanatory Reports Submitted to the International Socialist Congress of Stuttgart (18–24 August 1907)*. Hereafter *Propositions 1907*. For the specific resolutions:

Rules for International Congresses and the International Socialist Bureau

In English, *Propositions 1907*, pp. 397–400. In French, *Compte rendu 1907*, pp. 415–17. In German *Propositions 1907*, pp. 196–97.

Statutes of the Interparliamentary Commission

In English, *Propositions 1907*, pp. 401–3. In French, *Compte rendu 1907*, pp. 418–20. In German, *Propositions 1907*, pp. 197–99.

Militarism and International Conflicts

In English, *Second International Archives*, IISG. Also, *International Socialist Review* 8, no. 3, September 1907, pp. 135–37. In French, *Compte rendu 1907*, pp. 421–24. In German, *Protokoll 1907*, pp. 64–66.

The Relations between Trade Unions and Socialist Parties

In English, *International Socialist Review* 8, no. 3, September 1907, pp. 138–39. Also, *Second International Archives*, IISG. In French, *Compte rendu 1907*, pp. 424–26. In German, *Protokoll 1907*, pp. 50–51.

The Colonial Question

In English, *Second International Archives*, IISG. In French, *Compte rendu 1907*, pp. 426–28. In German, *Protokoll 1907*, pp. 39–40.

Immigration and Emigration of Workers

In English, *International Socialist Review* 8, no. 3, September 1907, pp. 139–41. Also, *Second International Archives*, IISG. In French, *Compte rendu 1907*, pp. 428–31. In German, *Protokoll 1907*, pp. 58–59.

Women's Suffrage

In English, *International Socialist Review* 8, no. 3, September 1907, p. 142. In French, *Compte rendu 1907*, pp. 431–32. In German, *Protokoll 1907*, p. 40.

On Romania

In English, *Second International Archives*, IISG. In French, *Compte rendu 1907*, pp. 432–33. In German, *Protokoll 1907*, p. 71.

Greetings to Revolutionaries of Russia

In French, *Compte rendu 1907*, p. 434. In German, *Protokoll 1907*, p. 71. For this book, translated from the French.

On Morocco

In French, *Compte rendu 1907*, p. 434. In German, *Protokoll 1907*, p. 72. For this book, translated from the French.

The Trial of the American Miners

In French, *Compte rendu 1907*, p. 435. In German, *Protokoll 1907*, p. 72. For this book, translated from the French.

8. COPENHAGEN CONGRESS OF 1910

Official proceedings: In French, *Huitième congrès socialiste international tenu à Copenhague du 28 août au 3 septembre 1910* (Brussels: Gand, Soc. Coop. "Volksdrukkerij"), hereafter *Compte rendu 1910*. In German, *Internationaler Sozialisten-Kongress zu Kopenhagen 28. August bis 3. September 1910* (Berlin: Verlag Buchhandlung Vorwärts, 1910), hereafter *Protokoll 1910*. In English most resolutions were published in *International Socialist Congress 1910* (Chicago: H. G. Adair printing, n.d.). For the specific resolutions:

The Unemployment Question

In English, *International Socialist Congress 1910*, p. 4. Also, *Second International Archives*, IISG. In French, *Compte rendu 1910*, pp. 461–62. In German, *Protokoll 1910*, pp. 56–57.

The Death Penalty

In English, *International Socialist Congress 1910*, pp. 4–5. Also, *Second International Archives*, IISG. In French, *Compte rendu 1910*, pp. 462–65. In German, *Protokoll 1910*, pp. 16–17.

Party Unity

In English, *International Socialist Congress 1910*, p. 7. Also, *Second International Archives*, IISG. In French, *Compte rendu 1910*, p. 462. In German, *Protokoll 1910*, p. 16.

War and Militarism

In English, *International Socialist Congress 1910*, pp. 10–11. Also, *Second International Archives*, IISG. In French, *Compte rendu 1910*, pp. 471–75. In German, *Protokoll 1910*, pp. 34–35.

On the Hardie-Vaillant Amendment

In English, *International Socialist Congress 1910*, p. 11. In French, *Compte rendu 1910*, p. 475. In German, *Protokoll 1910*, p. 35.

Carrying Out International Resolutions

In French, *Compte rendu 1910*, p. 475. In German, *Protokoll 1910*, p. 105. For this volume, translated from the French.

Trade Union Unity

In English, *International Socialist Congress 1910*, p. 12. In French, *Compte rendu 1910*, p. 476. In German, *Protokoll 1910*, p. 44.

International Solidarity

In English, *International Socialist Congress 1910*, pp. 12–13. Also, *Second International Archives*, IISG. In French, *Compte rendu 1910*, pp. 476–79. In German, *Protokoll 1910*, pp. 51–52.

Labor Legislation

In English, *International Socialist Congress 1910*, p. 14. Also, *Second International Archives*, IISG. In French, *Compte rendu 1910*, pp. 479–81. In German, *Protokoll 1910*, pp. 56–57.

The Right of Asylum

In English, *International Socialist Congress 1910*, p. 15. Also, *Second International Archives*, IISG. In French, *Compte rendu 1910*, pp. 483–84. In German, *Protokoll 1910*, p. 61.

On Cooperatives and Cooperation

In English, *International Socialist Congress 1910*, p. 15–16. Also, *Second International Archives*, IISG. In French, *Compte rendu 1910*, pp. 481–83. In German, *Protokoll 1910*, pp. 63–64.

On Japan

In English, *International Socialist Congress 1910*, p. 7. Also, *Second International Archives*, IISG. In French, *Compte rendu 1910*, pp. 466–67. In German, *Protokoll 1910*, p. 18.

On Argentina

In English, *Second International Archives*, IISG. In French, *Compte rendu 1910*, pp. 465–66. In German, *Protokoll 1910*, pp. 17–18.

The Situation in Turkey

In English, *International Socialist Congress 1910*, p. 7. Also, *Second International Archives*, IISG. In French, *Compte rendu 1910*, p. 468. In German, *Protokoll 1910*, pp. 19–20.

On Spain

In English, *International Socialist Congress 1910*, p. 8. Also, *Second International Archives*, IISG. In French, *Compte rendu 1910*, p. 467. In German, *Protokoll 1910*, p. 19.

On Persia

In English *International Socialist Congress 1910*, p. 8. Also, *Second International Archives*, IISG. In French, *Compte rendu 1910*, pp. 470–71. In German, *Protokoll 1910*, p. 20.

On Finland

In English, *International Socialist Congress 1910*, pp. 8–9. Also, *Second International Archives*, IISG. In French, *Compte rendu 1910*, pp. 468–70. In German, *Protokoll 1910*, pp. 18–19.

On Morocco

In French, *Compte rendu 1910*, pp. 484–85. In German, *Protokoll 1910*, p. 62. For this book, translated from the French.

9. BASEL CONGRESS OF 1912

Official proceedings. In German, *Ausserordentlicher Internationaler Sozialisten-Kongress zu Basel am 24. und 25. November 1912* (Berlin: Verlag Buchhandlung Vorwärts Paul Singer, 1912), hereafter *Protokoll 1912*. In French, *Compte rendu analytique du congrès socialiste international extraordinaire tenu à Bâle les 24 et 25 novembre 1912*, in *Bulletin Périodique du Bureau Socialiste International*, no. 10, n.d., hereafter *Compte rendu 1912*.

The Basel Manifesto on War and Militarism

In English, from *Bulletin Périodique du Bureau Socialiste International*, no. 10, pp. 9–12. In French, *Compte rendu 1912*, pp. 9–12. In German, *Protokoll 1912*, pp. 23–27.

APPENDIXES

Dutch Resolution on General Strike against War (1891)

In English, French, and German, *Second International Archives*, IISG.

French General Strike Resolution (1896)

In English, *Full Report of the Proceedings of the International Workers' Congress. London, July and August, 1896* (London, "The Labour Leader," 1896), p. 36. In English and French, *Second International Archives*, IISG.

Guesde-Ferri Resolution (1900)

In French, *Compte rendu 1900*, pp. 81–82. In German, *Protokoll 1900*, p. 19. For this book, translated from the French.

Adler-Vandervelde Resolution (1904)

In English: De Leon, *Flashlights 1904*, p. 98. In French, *Compte rendu 1904*, pp. 113–14. In German, *Protokoll 1904*, p. 63.

Majority Immigration Resolution (1904)

In French, *Compte rendu 1904*, pp. 118–19. In German, *Protokoll 1904*, pp. 50–51. For this book, translated from the French.

Minority Immigration Resolution (1904)

In English, *Flashlights 1904*, pp. 101–2. In German, *Protokoll 1904*, p. 51. In French, *Compte rendu 1904*, pp. 119–20.

Dutch Colonial Resolution (1904)

In International Socialist Bureau, *Internationales Sozialistisches Kongress / Congrès socialiste international / International Socialist Congress. Amsterdam 1904. Resolutionen / Résolutions / Resolutions* (Brussels, 1904): German, pp. 5–7; French, pp. 26–28; English, pp. 45–47.

Colonial Commission Majority Resolution (1907)

In English, *Second International Archives*, IISG. In French, *Compte rendu 1907*, pp. 227–28. In German, *Protokoll 1907*, p. 112.

American SP Resolution on Immigration (1907)

In English, *Propositions 1907*, pp. 557–58. In German, *Propositions 1907*, pp. 370–73. In French: *Compte rendu 1907*, pp. 230–31.

Luxemburg-Lenin-Martov Amendments to Militarism Resolution (1907)

In John Riddell, ed., *Lenin's Struggle for a Revolutionary International* (New York: Pathfinder Press, 1984), pp. 33–35.

Lenin's Resolution on Cooperatives (1910)

In Lenin, *Collected Works*, vol. 16, pp. 278–79.

GLOSSARY

Adler, Victor (1852–1918) – central leader of Austrian Social Democratic Party; prominent leader of Second International; supported Austro-Hungarian military effort in World War I; Austrian foreign minister 1918.

Anseele, Edward (1856–1938) – joined Belgian socialist movement 1870s; a founder of Belgian Workers Party; government minister after 1918.

Argyriadès, Paul (1849–1901) – originally from Greece; arrived in France as student 1871; joined French Workers Party early 1880s, later becoming member of Blanquist party.

Baader, Ottilie (1847–1925) – German women's rights activist and socialist beginning in late 1860s; founder of SPD women's office.

Bakunin, Mikhail (1814–1876) – Russian anarchist; leader of split with Marxist forces in First International.

Bebel, August (1840–1913) – a founder of German Social Democratic movement 1869; collaborator of Marx and Engels; SPD cochairperson from 1892 until his death; opposed revisionism in SPD and Second International, but came to adopt centrist position.

Beer, Max (1864–1943) – born in Austria; moved to Germany 1889 and joined SPD; London correspondent for *Vorwärts* 1902–1912; historian of British socialism; worked at Marx-Engels Institute in Moscow 1927–1929.

Bernstein, Eduard (1850–1932) – German Social Democrat; collaborator of Engels; theorist of revisionist current within socialist movement from 1898; member of centrist USPD during World War I; rejoined SPD 1919; Reichstag deputy 1902–1907, 1912–1918, 1920–1928.

Bertrand, Louis (1856–1943) – joined socialist movement 1870s; a founder of Belgian Workers Party 1885; founder and editor of *Le Peuple*; member of parliament 1894–1926.

Bissolati, Leonida (1857–1920) – founding member of Italian SP 1892; editor of *Avanti* 1896–1903, 1908–1910; expelled from SP 1912 for supporting Italy's war in Libya; founded Reformist Socialist Party, which supported Italy's entry into World War I; government minister 1916–1918.

Bohn, Frank (1878–1975) – Socialist Labor Party national secretary 1906–1908; joined SP 1908; supported US entry into World War I and broke with socialist movement 1917.

Bömelburg, Theodor (1862–1912) – joined SPD 1887; leader of German construction workers' union in Hamburg; member of Reichstag 1903–1912.

Bonnet, A. (1866–1933) – secretary of Internationalist Revolutionary Socialist Students in Paris 1891–1893; later participated in socialist publishing and educational efforts.

Bracke, Alexandre (1861–1955) – joined French socialist movement in 1880s, becoming leader of French SP and its foreign relations secretary; longtime member of Chamber of Deputies; supported French military effort during World War I.

Branting, Karl Hjalmar (1860–1925) – longtime leader of Swedish Social Democratic Party and editor of *Social-Demokraten* 1886–1917; supporter of Bernstein's revisionist perspective; opponent of Bolshevik revolution; chairperson of Second International 1919; three times prime minister 1920–1925.

Braun, Adolf (1862–1929) – a founder of Austrian Social Democratic Party 1887; moved to Germany; editor of *Vorwärts* 1893–1898; member of party executive 1920–1927.

Briand, Aristide (1862–1932) – a leader of French socialist movement and a founder of *L'Humanité*; became minister in bourgeois government 1906 and broke with socialist movement; premier of France numerous times between 1909 and 1929.

Brouckère, Louis de (1870–1951) – joined Belgian Workers Party early 1890s; left-wing socialist before 1914; supported Entente in World War I and joined Belgian government.

Brousse, Paul (1844–1912) – member of First International in France in 1870s as anarchist; later a reformist socialist and "Possibilist"; founding member of united French SP 1905.

Burrows, Herbert (1845–1922) – British socialist; founding member in 1881 of organization that became Social Democratic Federation, remaining a member until 1911.

Busche, J. Fred – leader of New Haven, Connecticut, typographical workers union in 1880s, serving as state deputy of union in 1882–1883; editor of

Socialist Labor Party's *Workmen's Advocate* 1887–1889; represented SLP at 1889 Second International congress, but was forced out of party in a faction fight later that year.

Cahan, Abraham (1860–1951) – born in Lithuania; emigrated to US 1882; joined Socialist Labor Party; later became member of SP; a founder in 1897 of Yiddish-language *Jewish Daily Forward* and its editor from 1903 to 1946.

Cipriani, Amilcare (1844–1918) – originally from Italy; moved to France 1870 and participated in Paris Commune; deported to New Caledonia 1871–1880; active in French and Italian socialist movements, influenced by anarchism; attended Second International congresses 1889, 1893, 1904; supported Entente in World War I.

Degay, Edmond (1862–1933) – Blanquist during 1890s; joined French Workers Party; delegate to 1893 and 1896 Second International congresses; subprefect of Molsheim (Bas-Rhin) 1919–1925.

de la Porte, Henri (1880–1924) – joined socialist student movement 1899; named to French SP National Council 1905; supported French war effort 1914; broke with SP 1919.

Delory, Gustave (1857–1925) – a founder of French textile workers union 1879; Socialist Party mayor of Lille 1896–1904 and 1919–1925; member of Chamber of Deputies 1902–1925.

de Paepe, César (1841–1890) – prominent member of First International in Belgium; moved from anarcho-syndicalism to Marxism; a founder of Belgian Workers Party; attended founding congress of Second International.

Drucker, Wilhelmina (1847–1925) – Dutch feminist and socialist; founder in 1889 of Free Women's Association, representing it at 1891 Second International congress.

Ebert, Friedrich (1871–1925) – joined SPD 1889; member of party executive committee 1905–1919; succeeded Bebel as party cochairman 1913; supported German effort in World War I; as a leader of provisional government coming out of 1918 revolution, he joined with monarchists to defeat workers' uprisings 1919–1920; German president 1919–1925.

Edwards, B. – member of Kommunistischer Arbeiterbildungsverein (Communist Workers Educational Association) in London.

Ellenbogen, Wilhelm (1863–1951) – founding member and prominent leader of Austrian Social Democratic Party; member of parliament 1901–1918; took pacifist position during World War I, participating in Zimmerwald movement; entered Social Democratic–led Austrian government in 1919.

Engels, Frederick (1820–1895) – lifelong collaborator of Karl Marx; coauthor of *Communist Manifesto*; a leader of First International 1864–1872; political and theoretical leader of revolutionary workers' movement after death of Marx; close adviser of Second International 1889–1895.

Ferrer, Francisco (1859–1909) – Catalan educator and anarchist; arrested, tried, and executed following Barcelona Tragic Week rebellion.

Ferri, Enrico (1856–1929) – Italian criminologist and socialist; joined Italian SP 1893; elected to Italian parliament 1896; editor of *Avanti* 1900–1905; became supporter of fascism under Mussolini.

Fière, Louis – revolutionary socialist militant in Drôme department of southeastern France.

Frankel, Leo (1844–1896) – member of First International; participant in Paris Commune; attended inaugural and subsequent congresses of Second International.

Friedeberg, Raphael (1863–1940) – German physician; joined SPD in 1890s; moved toward anarchism and became affiliated to Free Association of German Trade Unions; supported general strike motion at 1904 Amsterdam congress; expelled from SPD 1907 as anarcho-syndicalist.

Gérault-Richard, Alfred Léon (1860–1911) – joined French socialist movement 1880s; edited several socialist newspapers; member of parliament 1895–1898, 1902–1911; supported Millerand and bourgeois Republicans.

Gheude, Charles (1871–1956) – leading Belgian socialist and lawyer; Belgian Workers Party deputy 1907–1940; founder and editor in chief of *Jean Prolo* 1913–1956.

Gibson, Charles A. – member of Social Democratic Federation of Britain in 1890s; active in bus and cab drivers' union.

Glasier, J. Bruce (1859–1920) – founding member of Social Democratic Federation of Britain 1884, leaving it to join Socialist League; joined Independent Labour Party 1893; editor of *Labour Leader*; a founder of British Labour Party; took pacifist position during World War I.

Grantham, William (1835–1911) – British barrister, politician, and judge.

Gray, Mary (1854–1941) – joined Social Democratic Federation in Britain 1887; ran Socialist Sunday School; member of local SDF leadership 1896–1903.

Guérard, Eugène (1859–1931) – secretary of French National Railway Union 1890–1909, representing it at 1896 Second International congress.

Guesde, Jules (1845–1922) – veteran of Paris Commune and one of first Marxists in France; from 1882 leader of French Workers Party and French SP;

opponent of reformism until 1914; social patriot and minister of state without portfolio during World War I.

Hardie, Keir (1856–1915) – founding member of British Independent Labour Party, becoming a central party leader; a founder of Labour Party; member of Parliament 1892–1895, 1900–1915; adopted pacifist stand during World War I.

Haywood, William D. "Big Bill" (1869–1928) – elected secretary-treasurer of Western Federation of Miners in US 1900; founding member and first chairman of Industrial Workers of the World 1905; arrested 1917 on frame-up charges of treason and sabotage, convicted and sentenced to twenty years' imprisonment; jumped bail in 1921 and went to Soviet Russia, where he lived until his death.

Hennessey, Daniel – organizing secretary of British National Association of Operative Plasterers, representing it at 1896 Second International congress.

Hervé, Gustave (1871–1944) – joined French socialist movement 1899; led ultraleft tendency in SP before 1914; became prowar ultranationalist in 1914; expelled from SP 1916; sympathetic to fascism in 1920s; supported Vichy regime during World War II.

Hicks, Amie (1839/40? –1917) – president of British Rope Makers Union and member of Social Democratic Federation; founding member of Women's Trade Union Association, which became Women's Industrial Council.

Hillquit, Morris (1869–1933) – a founder and central leader of US SP from 1901; proponent of opportunist position on immigration question; supporter of centrist current within international Social Democracy.

Hobson, Samuel George (1870–1940) – member of British Fabian Society and Independent Labour Party; theorist of Guild Socialism.

Huggler, August (1877–1944) – secretary of Swiss metal workers union 1904–1909; secretary of Swiss trade union federation 1909–1915; remained a leader of federation until 1937.

Hunter, Robert (1874–1942) – American writer; author of *Poverty*; joined Socialist Party after 1905; delegate to 1907 and 1910 Second International congresses.

Huysmans, Camille (1871–1968) – joined Belgian Workers Party 1887; secretary of International Socialist Bureau from 1905; chairperson of Belgian House of Representatives 1936–1939, 1954–1958; Belgian prime minister 1946–1947.

Hyndman, Henry M. (1842–1921) – a founder in 1881 of what became Social Democratic Federation; helped establish British Socialist Party in 1911; noted for anti-Semitic views; supported British war effort during World War I; formed National Socialist Party in 1916.

Iglesias, Pablo (1850–1925) – founder of Spanish Social Democracy in 1879; president of SP 1888–1925; head of trade union federation; member of parliament 1910–1923; supported Entente during World War I.

Ihrer, Emma (1857–1911) – member of SPD in Germany; active in socialist women's movement from early 1880s; in 1891 founded *Die Arbeiterin*, predecessor of *Die Gleichheit*; later helped found German Central Association of Domestic Workers.

Jaclard, Charles Victor (1840–1903) – French socialist; member of First International as anarchist; participant in Paris Commune; lived in exile 1871–1880; active in French Workers Party; general secretary of Union of Socialist Journalists; delegate to Second International congresses of 1889, 1891, 1893.

Jankowska-Mendelson, Marya (1850–1909) – member of Polish league of revolutionary emigrants in London; later coeditor in Zurich of *Równość* (Equality); attended 1892 founding congress in Paris of Polish Socialist Party.

Jaurès, Jean (1859–1914) – socialist from late 1880s; leader of reformist wing of French Socialist movement; from 1905 a central leader of unified French SP; member of Chamber of Deputies 1888–1889, 1893–1898, 1902–1914; assassinated at outbreak of World War I.

Karpeles, Benno (1868–1938) – joined socialist movement in 1890s in Switzerland; moved to Vienna; became political editor of *Arbeiter-Zeitung* 1899; represented Austrian trade unions in Second International.

Karski – See Marchlewski, Julian.

Kautsky, Karl (1854–1938) – joined Austrian Social Democracy 1874; collaborator of Engels; chief editor of SPD journal *Die Neue Zeit* 1883–1917; prominent Marxist theorist and opponent of revisionism before 1914; centrist during World War I; opponent of October 1917 Russian Revolution and Communist movement.

Kautsky, Louise (1860–1950) – Austrian Social Democrat; Engels's secretary and housekeeper 1890–1895; an editor of *Arbeiterinnen-Zeitung*; member of bureau of 1893 Second International congress; first wife of Karl Kautsky.

Keufer, Auguste (1851–1924) – secretary general of French Federation of Book Workers 1884–1920; first treasurer of CGT union federation 1895–1896.

Knudsen, Peter (1848–1910) – leader of Danish SDP 1882–1910; member of Danish parliament 1898–1901 and 1902–1909.

Kulischioff, Anna (c. 1855–1925) – Russian revolutionary; fled from tsarist police; lived in Italy after 1878 and became active in socialist movement there; helped edit *Critica Sociale* from 1891; later a leader of reformist wing of Italian SP.

Lafargue, Paul (1842–1911) – member of General Council of First International; founding leader of French Workers Party 1880; a leader of Marxist left wing of French socialist movement; helped organize founding congress of Second International; son-in-law of Karl Marx.

Lanchester, Edith (1871–1966) – socialist, feminist, and suffragist; member of Social Democratic Federation, representing it at 1896 Second International congress.

Lang, Otto (1863–1936) – a founding leader of Swiss SDP 1888; chairperson of party 1899–1920; member of party leadership until his death.

Lansbury, George (1859–1940) – joined British Social Democratic Federation 1892; Labour Party member of Parliament 1910–1912, 1922–1940; Labour Party leader 1931–1935.

Lavigne, Raymond (1851–1930) – French syndicalist and socialist; leader of Bordeaux trade union movement from early 1880s; member of French Workers Party 1881–1902; made motion at 1889 Second International congress for May Day; joined unified SP 1905.

Leakey, James (b. 1849) – delegate to Second International's 1896 congress from British Independent Labour Party; author of *Co-operators and the Labour Platform*.

Ledebour, Georg (1850–1947) – joined SPD 1891; Reichstag member 1900–1918; supported SPD left wing before 1914; opposed social chauvinism during World War I; a leader of Independent Social Democratic Party (USPD) 1917–1919; opposed affiliation to Comintern 1920.

Lee, Algernon (1873–1954) – joined US Socialist Labor Party 1895; became a leader of SP after its founding in 1901; editor of *New York Call*.

Legien, Karl (1861–1920) – Social Democratic head of German trade unions 1890–1920; avowed reformist; president of International Federation of Trade Unions 1913–1919; supported SPD right wing during World War I.

Lenin, Vladimir Ilyich (1870–1924) – became active in Russian Social Democratic movement 1892–1893; central leader of Bolsheviks from 1903; became Bolshevik representative on International Socialist Bureau 1905; leader of October Revolution; chair of Soviet government 1917–1924; founder and leader of Communist International.

Liebknecht, Wilhelm (1826–1900) – participant in 1848 revolution in Germany; collaborator of Marx and Engels; cofounder of German Social

Democracy 1869 and, with Bebel, leader of SPD until his death; chief editor of *Vorwärts* 1876–1878 and 1891–1900.

Longuet, Jean (1876–1938) – joined French socialist movement 1890s; leader of centrists in SP during and after World War I; opposed affiliation to Comintern; parliamentary deputy 1914–1919 and 1932–1936; Karl Marx's grandson.

Louis, Paul (1872–1955) – joined French revolutionary movement 1888; became member of united SP 1901; member of its National Council from 1910; supported Russian Revolution and became member of Communist Party 1920.

Luxemburg, Rosa (1871–1919) – born in Poland; joined socialist movement 1886; later lived in Germany; delegate to all Second International congresses between 1896 and 1912; led SPD left wing in opposition to party right wing and, after 1910, against "Marxist Center" led by Kautsky; leader of Spartacus current during World War I; imprisoned 1916–1918; founding leader of German CP December 1918; arrested and murdered during workers' uprising in Berlin January 1919.

Marchand – French metalworker; member of Revolutionary Socialist Committee of Nantes; delegate to 1893 Zurich Congress.

Marchlewski, Julian (Karski) (1866–1925) – joined Social Democratic movement in Russian Poland 1889; joined Bolsheviks 1906; later active in German SPD; during World War I a leader of Spartacus group in Germany; played a leading role in Comintern.

Martov, Julius (1873–1923) – joined Russian social-democratic movement early 1890s; leader of Mensheviks from 1903; pacifist during World War I; in left wing of Mensheviks during 1917; opponent of October Revolution.

Marx, Eleanor (1855–1898) – joined Social Democratic Federation 1884, becoming member of Socialist League and later rejoining SDF; helped organize National Union of Gas Workers and General Labourers 1889; leading figure at congresses of Second International; daughter of Karl Marx.

Marx, Karl (1818–1883) – cofounder with Engels of modern communist workers' movement; leader of Communist League 1847–1852; coauthor of *Communist Manifesto*; central leader of First International 1864–1872.

Miller, Louis E. (1866–1927) – emigrated to US 1884, becoming leader of Jewish Workingmen's Association; represented Jewish Federation of Trade Unions of New York at Second International's 1889 congress; helped found socialist *Jewish Daily Forward* in 1897, but broke with it in 1905 and became a Zionist.

Millerand, Alexandre (1859–1943) – initially a leader of French SP; took ministerial post in cabinet 1899 and then moved to right of bourgeois political spectrum; French premier 1920; president 1920–1924.

Modráček, František (1871–1960) – originally an anarchist; joined Czechoslovak Social Democratic movement 1897; active in cooperative movement; member of Austro-Hungarian parliament 1907–1918; when party moved toward communism after war, he left to join Social Democrats; member of Czechoslovak senate 1925–1939.

Mojonnet, J. – secretary of French metalworkers union 1894; member of Revolutionary Socialist Workers Party, which became part of unified French SP.

Molkenbuhr, Hermann (1851–1927) – founding member of German Social Democratic Workers Party 1875; became secretary of SPD Executive Committee in 1904; represented SPD on International Socialist Bureau; supported right-wing party majority during World War I.

Morris, William (1834–1896) – British textile designer, writer, and poet; became Marxist in early 1880s; leader of Socialist League 1884–1890; later active in Hammersmith Socialist Society.

Mortier, B. – delegate from Saint-Étienne, France, representing National Federation of Metalworkers, at Second International congress in 1893.

Moyer, Charles (1866–1929) – president of Western Federation of Miners in US 1902–1926; charged in 1906 frame-up along with Haywood and Pettibone; charges against Moyer were eventually dropped.

Němec, Antonín (1858–1926) – joined workers' movement 1876; Czech SDP party chairperson and editor in chief of *Právo lidu* from 1897; helped lead struggle against party's pro-Communist left-wing majority.

Nieuwenhuis, Ferdinand Domela (1846–1919) – leader of Dutch socialist movement from 1879; advocated general strike against war at 1891 and 1893 International congresses; became anarchist and led split from Social Democracy in 1896.

Olsen, Christian Martin (1853–1926) – chairperson of Danish trade union federation 1903–1909; member of parliament 1901–1918; served on International Socialist Bureau.

Pankhurst, Richard (1834–1898) – London barrister; active in Liberal Party; founding member of British Independent Labour Party 1893, representing it at Second International's 1896 London Congress.

Pernerstorfer, Engelbert (1850–1918); joined Austrian SDP 1896, member of parliament 1885–1897, 1901–1918, becoming head of party's parliamentary group.

Pettibone, George (1862–1908) – member of Western Federation of Miners in Idaho; acquitted in 1907 frame-up trial.

Plekhanov, Georgy V. (1856–1918) – pioneer of Marxism in Russia; founder of Emancipation of Labor group 1883; influential Marxist theorist; supported Mensheviks after 1903; leading Russian representative at Second International congresses; supported Russian military effort during World War I; opposed October Revolution 1917.

Quelch, Harry (1858–1913) – leader of British Social Democratic Federation and British SP; editor of *Justice*, 1892–1913; attended all congresses of Second International from 1889 to 1910.

Rakovsky, Christian (1873–1941) – born in Bulgaria; driven into exile 1890, joining socialist movement in Switzerland; leading socialist activist in several European countries; took part in Zimmerwald conference 1915; joined Bolsheviks in Russia 1917; leader of Ukrainian soviet government 1919–1923; leader of Left Opposition in Russian CP 1923–1934; convicted in Moscow frame-up trial 1938; executed.

Rappoport, Charles (1865–1941) – born in Lithuania; joined Russian populist movement 1883; in exile from 1887; joined French socialist movement 1897; member French CP 1920–1938.

Rémy, Léon (1870–1910) – founder of Internationalist Revolutionary Socialist Students, representing it at 1893 and 1896 Second International congresses; a member of French SP at time of death.

Renou, Victor (1845–1904) – stonemason; participant in Paris Commune; founding member of French Workers Party 1880; later a member of Revolutionary Socialist Workers Party.

Roland-Holst, Henriette (1869–1952) – Dutch poet and writer; joined Dutch socialist movement 1897; active in work of Second International from 1900; belonged to left wing of Social Democratic Workers Party; founding member of Dutch Communist Party 1918; left CP 1927.

Rubanovich, I. A. (1860–1920) – a leader of Russian Socialist Revolutionary Party; member of International Socialist Bureau 1907–1909; supported Entente war effort during World War I.

Saint-Domingue – delegate to 1893 Zurich Congress from Proletarian Positivist Circle in Paris.

Savarkar, Vinayak Damodar (1883–1966) – Indian revolutionary nationalist; arrested in France 1910 and extradited; sentenced in British court to fifty years' imprisonment; released in 1924.

Schlüter, Hermann (1851–1919) – joined German Social Democracy 1872; emigrated to US 1889; contributor to *New Yorker Volkszeitung*; represented Socialist Party at 1904 Amsterdam Congress.

Serwy, Victor (1884–196?) – secretary of Belgian Cooperative Societies from 1900; secretary of Belgian Workers Party in Brussels; editor of *L'Avenir social*; secretary of International Socialist Bureau 1900–1905.

Simons, A. M. (1870–1950) – joined US Socialist Labor Party 1897; helped found SP 1901; editor *International Socialist Review* 1900–1908; supported US entry into World War I; later became supporter of Republican Party.

Singer, Paul (1844–1911) – joined German Social Democracy 1869; cochairperson of SPD Executive Committee 1890–1911; member of Reichstag 1884–1911; member of International Socialist Bureau; close collaborator of Bebel; opposed revisionist current within party and Second International.

Sorge, Friedrich Adolph (1828–1906) – friend and collaborator of Marx and Engels living in United States; became secretary of First International 1872; collaborator of *Die Neue Zeit* until death.

Stevenson, W. (b. 1854) – helped found United Builders Labourers' union in London; union general secretary 1889–1905.

Störmer, Albert (1847–1922) – leader of German sailors' union from Hamburg beginning 1891; resigned from trade union position 1903; later active in cooperative movement.

Thompson, Claude (born c. 1872) – secretary of Australian Rail and Tramway Service Association, representing this union at 1904 Amsterdam Congress; a leader of 1917 New South Wales general strike.

Troelstra, Pieter (1860–1930) – founding leader of Dutch Social Democratic Workers Party 1894; prominent opportunist within Second International; supported Entente during World War I.

Ugarte, Manuel (1875–1951) – joined Argentine Socialist Party 1903; left it 1913 due to party's rightist positions; a supporter of Latin American anti-imperialist movements; Argentine ambassador under Perón 1946–1950.

Vaillant, Édouard (1840–1915) – longtime French socialist; member General Council of First International and participant in Paris Commune; prominent antimilitarist favoring general strike to oppose war; supported French war effort in 1914.

Vandervelde, Émile (1866–1938) – leader of Belgian Workers Party; chairperson of Brussels office of Second International 1900–1914; member of Belgian council of ministers 1916–1921, 1925–1927, 1936–1937; chairperson of Belgian Workers Party 1933–1938.

Van Kol, Hendrick (1852–1925) – member of First International; lived many years in Dutch East Indies; founding leader of Dutch Social Democratic Workers Party; prominent opportunist on colonial and other questions within Second International.

Verdorst, Pieter Marinus (1858–1944) – joined Dutch trade union movement 1887; became chairman of carpenters union 1890s; a founder of Trade Union Association (NVV) 1906 and member of its executive board until 1920.

Vinck, Émile (1870–1950) – a leader of Belgian Workers Party; secretary of National Federation of Communal Socialist Councilors and founder of its newspaper, *Le Mouvement Communal*.

Vliegen, Willem H. (1862–1947) – founding leader of Dutch Social Democratic Workers Party 1894, becoming party chairperson and editor of its central organ; leading reformist; member of Dutch parliament 1909–1937.

Volders, Jean (1855–1896) – a founding leader of Belgian Workers Party 1885; editor in chief of *Le Peuple*.

von Elm, Adolph (1857–1916) – a leader of German cooperative movement; joined Social Democracy 1870s; president of tobacco workers cooperative in Hamburg 1891–1912; Reichstag member 1894–1907; founder and leader of trade union insurance company 1910–1916.

von Plehve, Vyacheslav (1846–1904) – minister of interior and head of police in tsarist Russia 1902; aided and abetted anti-Jewish pogroms; assassinated by revolutionaries.

Webb, Sidney (1859–1947) – leading figure in British Fabian Society; colonial minister in Labour Party government, 1929–1931.

Wibaut, Florentinus Marinus (1858–1936) – leading member of Dutch Social Democratic Workers Party; centrist before 1914, then right-wing Social Democrat.

Wurm, Emmanuel (1857–1920) – joined German SPD 1880s; leading supporter with Kautsky of SPD "Marxist Center"; Reichstag deputy from 1890; supporter of centrist opposition within SPD after 1915; founding member of Independent Social Democratic Party; Prussian food minister 1918.

Zetkin, Clara (1857–1933) – joined German socialist movement 1878; cofounder of Second International 1889; a leader of its Marxist wing; editor of SPD's women's journal *Die Gleichheit* 1891–1917; campaigner for women's emancipation; secretary of International Socialist Women's Bureau from 1907; joined German CP 1919; headed Communist Women's Movement 1921–1926; founder and editor of *Die Kommunistische Fraueninternationale* 1921–1925; member Executive Committee of Communist International 1921–1933; Reichstag member 1920–1933.

INDEX

ABOUT HAYMARKET BOOKS

Haymarket Books is a radical, independent, nonprofit book publisher based in Chicago.

Our mission is to publish books that contribute to struggles for social and economic justice. We strive to make our books a vibrant and organic part of social movements and the education and development of a critical, engaged, international left.

We take inspiration and courage from our namesakes, the Haymarket martyrs, who gave their lives fighting for a better world. Their 1886 struggle for the eight-hour day—which gave us May Day, the international workers' holiday—reminds workers around the world that ordinary people can organize and struggle for their own liberation. These struggles continue today across the globe—struggles against oppression, exploitation, poverty, and war.

Since our founding in 2001, Haymarket Books has published more than five hundred titles. Radically independent, we seek to drive a wedge into the risk-averse world of corporate book publishing. Our authors include Noam Chomsky, Arundhati Roy, Rebecca Solnit, Angela Y. Davis, Howard Zinn, Amy Goodman, Wallace Shawn, Mike Davis, Winona LaDuke, Ilan Pappé, Richard Wolff, Dave Zirin, Keeanga-Yamahtta Taylor, Nick Turse, Dahr Jamail, David Barsamian, Elizabeth Laird, Amira Hass, Mark Steel, Avi Lewis, Naomi Klein, and Neil Davidson. We are also the trade publishers of the acclaimed Historical Materialism Book Series and of Dispatch Books.